Heartbreak to Hope

Good news from Mark

Let your heartbreak, pain and uncertainty be overcome by Christ's hope, healing and love.

MELANIE NEWTON

We extend our heartfelt thanks to the women's ministry team at RockPointe Church for giving us the opportunity to develop and lead this study for women during the spring of 2018. Many thanks also to the women in the classes who helped me to sharpen the discussion surrounding this study of Mark, especially Susan Lewis, Marlo Brazeal, and Connie Crowley.

© 2024 Melanie Newton. Published by Joyful Walk Press. All rights reserved.

For questions about the use of this study guide, please contact us at melanienewton.com.

Cover graphic adapted from an image provided on canva.com.

Scripture quotations unless otherwise noted are taken from the Holy Bible, New International Version ®, NIV ®. Copyright © 1973, 1978, 1984 by International Bible Society. Used by permission of Zondervan Publishing Company. All rights reserved.

Scripture quotations indicated NET are quoted by permission from the NET Bible® copyright ©1996-2006 by Biblical Studies Press, L.L.C. www.bible.org All rights reserved. This material is available in its entirety as a free download or online web use at http://netbible.org.

Melanie Newton is the author of "Graceful Beginnings" books for anyone new to the Bible and "Joyful Walk Bible Studies" for established Christians. Her mission is to help women learn to study the Bible for themselves and to grow their Bible-teaching skills to lead others. For questions about the use of this study guide, please visit melanienewton.com to contact us.

Joyful Walk Bible Studies are grace-based studies for women of all ages. Each study guide follows the inductive method of Bible study (observation, interpretation, application) in a warm and inviting format. We pray that you and your group will find *Heartbreak to Hope: Good News from Mark* a resource that God will use to strengthen you in your faith walk with God.

Christ-Focused • Grace-Based • Bible-Rich

JOYFUL WALK PRESS
Flower Mound, TX

MELANIE NEWTON

Melanie Newton is a Louisiana girl who made the choice to follow Jesus while attending LSU. She and her husband Ron married and moved to Texas for him to attend Dallas Theological Seminary. They stayed in Texas where Ron led a wilderness camping ministry for troubled youth for many years. Ron now helps corporations with their challenging employees and is the author of the top-rated business book, *No Jerks on the Job*.

Melanie jumped into raising three Texas-born children and serving in ministry to women at her church. Through the years, the Lord has given her opportunity to do Bible teaching and to write grace-based Bible studies for women that are now available from her website (melanienewton.com) and on Bible.org. *Graceful Beginnings* books are for anyone new to the Bible. *Joyful Walk Bible Studies* are for maturing Christians.

Melanie Newton loves to help women learn how to study the Bible for themselves. She also teaches online courses for women to grow their Bible-teaching skills to help others—all with the goal of getting to know Jesus more along the way. Her heart's desire is to encourage you to have a joyful relationship with Jesus Christ so you are willing to share that experience with others around you.

"Jesus took hold of me in 1972, and I've been on this great adventure ever since. My life is a gift of God, full of blessings in the midst of difficult challenges. The more I've learned and experienced God's absolutely amazing grace, the more I've discovered my faith walk to be a joyful one. I'm still seeking that joyful walk every day..."

Melanie

OTHER BIBLE STUDIES BY MELANIE NEWTON

Graceful Beginnings Series books for anyone new to the Bible:
A Fresh Start (basics for new Christians)
Painting the Portrait of Jesus (the Gospel of John)
The God You Can Know (the character of God)
Grace Overflowing (an overview of Paul's 13 letters)
The Walk from Fear to Faith (7 Old Testament women)
Satisfied by His Love (women who knew Jesus)
Seek the Treasure (study of Ephesians)
Pathways to a Joyful Walk (6 pathways to a joy-filled life)

Joyful Walk Bible Studies for growing Christians:
Adorn Yourself with Godliness (1 Timothy and Titus, also in Spanish)
Everyday Women, Ever Faithful God (Old Testament women, also in Spanish)
Connecting Faith to Life on Planet Earth (Genesis 1-11; Revelation)
Graceful Living (the essentials for a grace-based Christian life)
Graceful Living Today (a devotional journal for a joyful life)
Healthy Living (Colossians and Philemon)
Heartbreak to Hope (the Gospel of Mark)
Identity: Sticking to Your Faith in a Pull-Apart World (Ezra thru Malachi)
Knowing Jesus, Knowing Joy (Philippians, also in Spanish)
Live Out His Love (New Testament women)
Perspective (1 and 2 Thessalonians)
Profiles of Perseverance (Old Testament men, also in Spanish)
Radical Acts (Acts)
Reboot, Renew, Rejoice (1 and 2 Chronicles)
The God-Dependent Woman (2 Corinthians)
To Be Found Faithful (2 Timothy)

Bible Study Leadership Courses
Be a Christ-Focused Small Group Leader
Leap into Lifestyle Disciplemaking
Bible Study Leadership Made Easy (online video course)
Painting the Picture of Jesus (the "I Am's" of Jesus lessons for children)
Teaching Children the God They Can Know (the character of God for children)

Download our catalogue and get resources for your spiritual growth at melanienewton.com.

Contents

Using This Study Guide 1

Lesson 1: Silence Is Broken at Last! 7

Lesson 2: Friends, Family, and Fast-spreading News 19

Lesson 3: Forgiving, Calling, Claiming, & Appointing 29

Lesson 4: Blasphemy, Parables, and a Stormy Night 41

Lesson 5: Desperation, Deliverance, and Deli on Command 51

Lesson 6: Clean, Unclean & Being "All In" or Nothing 65

Lesson 7: Glory, Honesty, & Serious Pride Issues 77

Lesson 8: A Parade, Housecleaning, and Lots of Tests! 89

Lesson 9: Prophecy, Perfume and Passover 101

Lesson 10: Facing the Giants 113

Lesson 11: He Is Alive! Hope Springs New 125

Preview of "Radical Acts" 137

The Miracles of Jesus in Mark 151

Principles on Marriage and Divorce 153

Whatever Happened to the Twelve Apostles? 156

Sources 157

Using This Study Guide

This study guide consists of 11 Lessons covering the gospel of Mark. Since Mark consists of 16 chapters, we will need to cover more than one chapter in most of the lessons. The lessons are divided into 5 sections (about 25 minutes in length). The first 4 sections contain a detail study of the passages. The last section is a podcast that provides additional insight to the lesson.

If you cannot do the entire lesson one week, please read the Bible passage covered by the lesson and try to do the "Day One Study" of the lesson.

THE BASIC STUDY

Each Lesson includes core questions covering the passage narrative. These core questions will take you through the process of inductive Bible study—observation, interpretation, and application. The Inductive process is the best way to study the Bible. The process is more easily understood in the context of answering these questions:

- ✓ What does the passage say? *(Observation: what's actually there)* **Discover the Facts** questions are the observation questions in this study.

- ✓ What does it mean? *(Interpretation: the author's intended meaning, leading to what it means for us today)*

- ✓ How does this apply to me today? *(Application: making it personal)* **Heartbreak to Hope** questions are the application questions in this study. These questions will lead you to introspection and application of a specific truth to your life.

STUDY ENHANCEMENTS

To aid in proper interpretation and application of the study, five additional study aids are located where appropriate in the Lesson:

- ✓ Historical Insights
- ✓ Scriptural Insights
- ✓ From the Greek/Hebrew (definitions of Greek or Hebrew words)
- ✓ Focus on the Meaning
- ✓ Think About It (thoughtful reflection)

Other useful study tools: Use online tools or apps (blueletterbible.org or "Blue Letter Bible app" is especially helpful) to find *cross references* (verses with similar content to what you are studying) and meanings of the *original Greek words or phrases* used (usually called "interlinear"). You can also look at any verse in *various Bible translations* to help with understanding what it is saying. Feel free to add your own study at the end of each lesson.

PODCASTS

Find podcasts for these lessons at melanienewton.com/podcasts (choose "10: Mark) and on most podcast providers. Or you can read the blogs associated with the podcasts at melanienewton.com/blog. Choose Mark category then scroll to find the title you want. Listen to the first podcast as an introduction to the study.

BIBLE BASICS

The Bible is one book containing a collection of 66 books combined together for our benefit. It is divided into two main parts: Old Testament and New Testament.

The Old Testament tells the story of the beginning of the world and God's promises to mankind given through the nation of Israel. All the stories and messages in the Old Testament lead up to Jesus Christ's coming to the earth.

The New Testament tells the story of Jesus Christ, the early Christians, and God's promises to all those who believe in Jesus. You can think of the Old Testament as "before Christ" and the New Testament as "after Christ."

Each book of the Bible is divided into chapters and verses within those chapters to make it easier to study. Verses are like line numbers. Not in the original writings. Bible references include the book name, chapter number and verse number(s). For example, Mark 12:28 refers to the New Testament book of Mark, the 12th chapter, and verse 28 within that 12th chapter. Printed Bibles have a "Table of Contents" in the front to help you locate books by page number. Bible apps for your phone or tablet also have a contents list by book and chapter.

We will be mostly in the New Testament. It was originally written in Greek. We primarily used the NIV® (New International Version) in the preparation of these Lessons. I recommend that you use one of the more direct English translations of the Bible for your personal study (i.e., NIV, ESV, NAS, NET, NKJ). The NLT (New Living Translation) and the MSG (The Message) versions use modern everyday language to illustrate what a passage is saying and can help you to understand difficult passages. You can find all these translations in most Bible Apps or online at various websites such as biblegateway.com and Bible.com.

This study capitalizes certain pronouns referring to God, Jesus and the Holy Spirit—He, Him, His, Himself—just to make the reading of the study information less confusing. Some Bible translations likewise capitalize those pronouns referring to God; others do not. It is simply a matter of preference, not a requirement.

NEW TESTAMENT SUMMARY

The New Testament opens with the births of John (the Baptist) and Jesus. About 30 years later, John challenged the Jews to indicate their repentance (turning from sin and toward God) by submitting to water baptism—a familiar Old Testament practice used for repentance as well as when a Gentile (non-Jew) converted to Judaism (to be washed clean of idolatry).

Jesus, God's incarnate Son, publicly showed the world what God is like and taught His perfect ways for 3 – 3½ years. After preparing 12 disciples to continue Christ's earthly work, He died voluntarily on a cross for mankind's sin, rose from the dead, and returned to heaven.

The account of Jesus' earthly life is recorded in 4 books known as the Gospels (the biblical books of Matthew, Mark, Luke and John named after the compiler of each account).

After Jesus' return to heaven, the followers of Christ were then empowered by the Holy Spirit and spread God's salvation message among the Jews, a number of whom believed in Christ. The apostle Paul and others carried the good news to the Gentiles during 3 missionary journeys (much of this recorded in the book of Acts).

Paul wrote 13 New Testament letters to churches & individuals (Romans through Philemon). The section in our Bible from Hebrews to Jude contains 8 additional letters penned by five men, including two apostles (Peter and John) and two of Jesus' half-brothers (James and Jude). The author of Hebrews is unknown.

The apostle John also recorded Revelation, a summary of God's final plan for our world. The Bible ends as it began with a new, sinless creation.

Discussion Group Guidelines

1. **Attend consistently** whether your Lesson is done or not. You'll learn from the other women, and they want to get to know you.
2. **Set aside time** to work through the study questions. The goal of Bible study is to get to know Jesus. He will change your life.
3. **Share your insights** from your personal study time. As you spend time in the Bible, Jesus will teach you truth through His Spirit inside you.
4. **Respect each other's insights**. Listen thoughtfully. Encourage each other as you interact. Refrain from dominating the discussion if you have a tendency to be talkative. ☺
5. **Celebrate our unity** in Christ. Avoid bringing up controversial subjects such as politics, divisive issues, and denominational differences.
6. **Maintain confidentiality.** Remember that anything shared during the group time is not to leave the **group** (unless permission is granted by the one sharing).
7. **Pray for one another** as sisters in Christ.
8. **Get to know the women** in your group. Please do not use your small group members for solicitation purposes for home businesses, though.

Enjoy your Joyful Walk Bible Study!

INTRODUCTION

PODCAST LISTENER GUIDE

> **Recommended:** Listen to the podcast "God Works in the Background of Life" before doing the first lesson as an introduction to the whole study.

God Works in the Background of Life

Before Jesus came, there had been 400 years of "silence" from God. No prophets had been speaking or writing anything from God to the people during that time. But in that time, God was at work in the background to prepare the way for answering the prayers of His people for deliverance.

THE PRESENCE OF THE SYNAGOGUE

- In 586 BC, Israel found herself in exile in Babylon because of her idolatry. The Jews carried their scriptures with them, especially the Torah. They met together in community groups for worship and reading of their Scriptures in what we now know as synagogues.

- As a result, Judaism became a faith that could be practiced wherever the Torah scrolls could be carried. This helped to preserve Judaism and prepare the way for the Christian gospel. By Jesus' time, Jews filled every land around the Mediterranean Sea.

- Synagogues were built all over the Greek and Roman world among the Gentile or non-Jewish people. The Jews shared the knowledge of the living and true God in their weekly worship times as God-fearing Gentiles would join them to worship God.

- The missionaries of the early church began their ministries among those dispersed Jews, using the weekly synagogue meetings as the platform for sharing the good news about Jesus to the Jews present as well as those God-fearing Gentiles.

- God was at work in the background to prepare the way for answering the prayers of the people for their Messiah to come to deliver them. And part of His work included the dispersion of Jews in the Roman Empire and the development of the synagogue.

THE EASE OF A COMMON LANGUAGE

- After Alexander the Great's conquests, Greek language and culture spread to all the conquered territories. Most people in the Mediterranean world learned to speak and write Greek. The Old Testament was translated into Greek (the Septuagint).

- Paul and other New Testament writers wrote in Greek which could be read everywhere in those countries influenced by the Greek culture.

ROMAN ROADS AND "PEACE"

- In the century before Jesus was born, Rome conquered Israel and the rest of the countries surrounding the Mediterranean.

- They brought "peace" to the whole region, although it was a forced peace. Law and order prevailed. Anyone who rebelled was quickly squashed by the powerful Roman army.

- The Romans built a system of roads so people could travel from the farthest reaches of the Empire back to mother Rome. Paul and the other missionaries of the first century utilized these roads for their travel as well as available sea travel.

BABIES MUST BE BORN AND GROW UP.

- Thirty years before the Jewish people as a nation finally heard from God again, the angel Gabriel delivered the message to two people that their sons would be the ones through whom God would answer the prayers of His people for deliverance.

- But before that happened, the babies had to be born, experience childhood, and grow up into men prepared to do their work. That took 30+ more years of waiting. Only a few people knew what was going on during this time. And they did not really understand it. But they did their part in the preparation.

- John the Baptist appeared on the scene at the appointed time in God's plan. Jesus left his father's carpentry shop a short time later and began His full-time ministry of teaching the people about getting ready for the Kingdom of God to come to them and healing their diseases.

- Through normal human birth and development, God was at work in the background to prepare the way for answering the prayers of all people for deliverance. He gets your need for hope.

THE NEED FOR HOPE

- God looked upon your life with compassion and provided a solution—His Son Jesus Christ. God in the flesh. God on earth. The God of hope and love.

- Jesus experienced human life for more than 30 years. He understands every single one of your heartaches because those were part of His life as well. When you go to Him in prayer, you can trust that He understands how you are feeling and what your are needing.

GOD IS STILL AT WORK IN THE BACKGROUND OF LIFE.

Can you look back now and recognize how God was at work on your behalf or for someone you love? Praise Him for that. Are you still waiting for God to answer a specific prayer of yours? Maybe our faithful God is preparing the background for answering your prayer tomorrow. Trust Him.

Let Jesus satisfy your heart with hope, healing, and love as you get to know Him and trust Him more each day.

Lesson 1: Silence Is Broken at Last!

DAY ONE STUDY

Ask the Lord Jesus to speak to you through His Word. Tell Him that you are listening.

The ABCs of Mark—Author, Background, and Context

Like any book you read, it always helps to know a bit about the author, the background setting for the story (i.e., past, present, future), and where the book fits into a series (that's the context). The same is true of Bible books.

AUTHOR — JOHN MARK

Since earliest times, John Mark was known to be the author of this gospel. It was common at the time for Jews to have two names. John was his Hebrew name; Mark was his Greek/Roman name. It is thought that he was from a wealthy family. In Mark 14:51-52, Mark may have written a veiled reference to himself since no other gospel writer mentions this incident. He describes a young man, likely a teenager, in a linen garment (his underwear, evidence of being wealthy) who followed Jesus out to the Garden of Gethsemane.

Mark was part of the Jerusalem church community, where he listened to the apostles' teaching. At times, the church would gather at his mother's house to pray. About 11 years after the resurrection, Mark left Jerusalem with his cousin Barnabas to go to Antioch in Syria. There, Barnabas and Paul headed up a growing church filled with non-Jews ("Gentiles").

Two years later, Mark traveled with Barnabas and Paul on their first missionary journey to Cyprus. A year later, when they got to what we know as southern Turkey, Mark left them and headed back to Jerusalem. We do not know the reasons behind his departure.

Three years later (as a 30-something), Barnabas and Paul were planning to head out on their second missionary trip. Barnabas wanted to take his cousin Mark. Paul said no, remembering how Mark had deserted them. Barnabas wanted to continue mentoring his cousin so he took Mark with him to Cyprus again. Paul took Silas and headed north to Turkey.

For the next 15-20 years, Mark traveled with Peter, listening to Peter's sermons and recording them. Peter probably had the greatest influence on Mark. When Mark was around 50, an aging Peter calls him "my son" in the letter we know as 1 Peter, written from Rome.

By this time, Mark's relationship with Paul was restored. Both times when Paul is in prison in Rome, Mark is there with him. Paul calls Mark his fellow worker and very useful to him. It is generally believed that Mark adapted Peter's preaching and teachings about Jesus into the book we now call "Mark," arranged and shaped as he was guided by the Holy Spirit. So the young teen who knew Jesus as a youth had many experiences that shaped his life and led him to the work that God had in mind for him. (References to Mark in the New Testament are found in Acts 12:12; 13:4-5, 13; 15:36-41; Colossians 4:10-11; 2 Timothy 4:9-11 and 1 Peter 5:13)

BACKGROUND — WRITTEN FROM ROME TO ROMAN GENTILE CHRISTIANS

Since Mark was with both Peter and Paul in Rome, we can be confident that he wrote his book from there. Most of the Roman Christians were non-Jews (Gentiles) who were definitely not familiar with the Old Testament and spoke Latin, not Hebrew. So Mark uses Latin terms, explains Jewish customs, and leaves out Old Testament quotes and genealogies. He also explains the Aramaic words that Jesus spoke (similar to Hebrew).

The Romans were designers, engineers, doers, slaveholders, soldiers, conquerors, and partiers. Because they were such action-oriented people, Mark writes in an action style. He frequently uses the words "immediately" and "right away"—7 times in chapter 1 alone. He writes mostly in the present tense when relating the stories of Christ so it feels like they are happening right now. He uses descriptive words and paints vivid word pictures so it feels like you are there in the crowd. In fact, because Mark briefly describes scenes and activities, he is called the photographer of the gospels. Each section of writing is like a snapshot from Jesus' life. Think slideshow, Facebook or Instagram.

Mark was aware of the suffering that the Roman Christians were beginning to experience under the Roman Emperor named Nero—a cruel, crazy guy. This book was written when persecution against Christians was just starting in Nero's reign. There are lots of references to suffering throughout Mark.

Context — Where It Fits into the Bible

When you look at your Bible's table of contents, the first 4 books of the New Testament—Matthew, Mark, Luke and John—are called the "Gospels" (meaning "good news," referring to the good news about Jesus). The Gospels tell of the life of Jesus from different perspectives. Mark is thought to be the first gospel written though it's not listed first in the New Testament. Matthew and Luke were written a couple of years after Mark and share a lot of the same content. John was written after all three.

The basic outline of Mark can be found in Peter's sermon from Acts 10:36-43—John's baptism, Jesus' miracles and teaching, the crucifixion, the resurrection, then go and tell the good news.

Mark answers two significant questions in his writing: 1) Who is Jesus? 2) How can I follow Jesus even when it's tough?

1. What grabbed your attention as you read the ABC's of the book of Mark?

Heartbreak to Hope

This world is full of heartache and pain. Human distress is everywhere around us. Chronic illness. Persecution. Poverty. Unrealized dreams. Job struggles. Women and men are in bondage to guilt, fear, destructive behavior, and fatigue due to the burden of responsibilities. Broken relationships leave people with a sense of rejection, worthlessness and extreme loneliness. Add to those any feelings of uncertainty often revealed by the questions we ask about life. "When will I _____ (make a friend, find love, get married, have a baby, get a better job, etc.)?" "What will I do after _____ (graduation, my children grow up, this job ends, etc.)?" Where do you go for help?

Sadly, if you have been taught that God does not care or is punishing you for something you have done wrong, you are not likely to trust Him for help. This may leave you feeling empty, confused, and without meaning and purpose. The Bible describes that as being *"without hope and without God in the world"* (Ephesians 2:12). Hopeless. Godless. A miserable existence characterized by heartbreak. But God looked upon your life with compassion and provided a solution—His Son Jesus Christ. God in the flesh. God on earth. The God of hope and love.

Jesus understands every single one of your heartaches. He experienced human life for more than 30 years. He gets your physical pain, rejection, strained relationships, abuse, grief, and impatience because those were part of His life as well. When you go to Him in prayer, you can trust that He understands, that He knows how you are feeling and what your needs are at that moment.

Jesus interacted with men and women everywhere He went. And there were so many who had heartaches and pain, filled with uncertainty about their future. Jesus looked upon the crowds of people with compassion. He not only felt their need but also wanted to do something about it. Jesus Christ's plan to meet that need for every person was then, and is now, Himself.

Jesus is the light that gives you hope for every heartbreak that you experience.

> All around us it is easy to see the darkness present in this world. Wickedness, greed, selfishness, cold-blooded violence... the darkness can quickly overwhelm a soul. But there is hope! Isaiah 9:2 predicted that those living in darkness would see a great light. Jesus was that light. And when you look at His life in the Gospel books you can see that He broke the darkness that was present in His land. He healed sick people, taught the curious how to live a life of purpose, and forgave the sins of those who were longing to be free from their guilt. He still does the same today. Our world is not completely dark. There is light that always dawns. (John Newton, *Advent for Restless Hearts,* p. 18)

Through this study of the gospel of Mark you will learn about Jesus' life on earth, how He related to people and why knowing Him brings hope to your life. Let your heartbreak, pain and uncertainty be overcome by Christ's hope, healing and love.

> *May the God of hope fill you with all joy and peace as you trust in Him, so that you may overflow with hope by the power of the Holy Spirit. (Romans 15:13)*

2. What heartaches do you have right now? What is causing you pain? Where is your uncertainty?

Ask Jesus to overcome your heartbreak, pain and uncertainty with His hope, healing and love as you learn from the gospel of Mark.

Process of Bible Study

The inductive process is the best way to study the Bible. It includes 3 elements:

- *Observation*: What does it say? (What is in the biblical text as you read it) **Discover the Facts** questions in this study are observation questions.
- *Interpretation*: What does it mean? (The author's intended meaning to his audience, leading to what it means for us today)
- *Application*: What application can you make to life today? (What you learn personally) **Heartbreak to Hope** questions in this study are application questions.

We will spend a lot of our time on observation—seeing what is actually there. Sometimes, we will seek understanding of the author's intended meaning through additional study. You want to understand the passage before you try to apply it. It helps to have access to great resources to help with interpretation. Here are some online study resources that I use and can recommend.

- gotquestions.org (write out your question, follow "rabbit trails")
- bible.org (search for more detail about subjects)
- blueletterbible.org or Blue Letter Bible app (translation comparisons, Greek word meanings, cross references)
- soniclight.com (check out Dr. Constable's Study Notes on Mark)

Respond to the Lord about what He's shown you today.

Day Two Study

Ask the Lord Jesus to speak to you through His Word. Tell Him that you are listening.

3. Recall a time when you announced the good news that something, for which you had been waiting a long time, was finally going to take place. What was the news? Whom did you tell? How did you feel?

Setting the Stage

During the 600 years before the birth of Jesus, the Jewish people had gone through a lot of harsh experiences. After being sent by God to exile in Babylon for 70 years, they came back to their land only to be ruled by other nations—Persia, Greece, Egypt and Syria respectively. The last rulers were especially cruel. Some Jews revolted which led to about 100 years of independence. Then, Rome conquered the nation. By the time Jesus began His public ministry, Israel had been under Roman rule for 90 years. The people were impatient to get out of their bondage to Rome.

There had also been 400 years of "silence" from God. No prophets had been speaking or writing anything from God to the people during that time. But the last Old Testament prophet Malachi had promised this:

> "I will send my messenger, who will prepare the way before me. Then suddenly the Lord you are seeking will come to his temple; the messenger of the covenant, whom you desire, will come," says the Lord Almighty...See, I will send the prophet Elijah to you." (Malachi 3:1; 4:5).

As the New Testament opens, Israel's king was Herod the Great who was not of Jewish descent. The Jewish priesthood was politically appointed and no longer from the God-chosen line of Aaron. The overall mood of the people was one of despondency because they felt like they were still in captivity.

Yet, good things were happening to prepare the way for Jesus. Synagogues, community places of worship that developed during the Exile, had sprouted up all over the country making weekly worship accessible to all the people. The Old Testament scriptures were translated into Greek, the common language of the Roman Empire, so were more accessible to all communities of people where Jews met together. And God soon ended the 400 years of silence in a big way although only a few people knew what was happening.

4. Skim Luke 1 and 2. During the 30 years before the Jewish people as a nation finally heard from Him again, what was God at work doing?

Read Mark 1:1-13.

God breaks His silence by sending a prophet named John. We know him as John the Baptist, the one who prepared the way for Israel's Messiah to be revealed.

5. Right away in verse 1, how does Mark answer the question, "Who is Jesus?" [Note: We'll see it answered twice more in this Lesson.]

> **Scriptural Insight:** *Messiah* comes from the Hebrew word *mashiach,* meaning "anointed one" or "chosen one." The Greek equivalent is the word *Christos* or, in English, *Christ.* The name "Jesus Christ" is the same as "Jesus the Messiah." In biblical times, anointing with oil was a sign that God was consecrating that person for a particular role. Thus, an "anointed one" was someone with a special, God-ordained purpose. The Jews of Jesus' day expected the Messiah to redeem Israel by overthrowing the rule of the Romans and establishing an earthly kingdom. It wasn't until after Jesus' resurrection that His disciples finally began to understand that the Messiah would first deliver His people *spiritually*; that is, to redeem them from sin. Later, Jesus the Messiah will deliver His people from their physical enemies, when He sets up His Kingdom on the earth. ("What does Messiah mean?" accessed at www.gotquestions.org)

6. ***Discover the Facts:*** Let's focus on vv. 1-8 today. The following questions will help you answer the observation question, "What does it say?"

What does God promise to send (v. 2)?

For whom is the messenger preparing the way (v. 3)?

HEARTBREAK TO HOPE: GOOD NEWS FROM MARK

Knowing this, who is John?

What is John doing in the wilderness (v. 4)?

Who is coming to the wilderness (v. 5)?

What did John wear and eat (v. 6)?

What was also his message (vv. 7-8)?

7. John is preaching a baptism of repentance for the forgiveness of sins. Let's define these words.

- What does the word *baptism* mean?

- What does the word *repentance* mean?

- What does the word *forgiveness* mean?

Focus on the Meaning: The word *baptism* carried with it the picture of both cleansing and identification. When Gentiles chose to become Jews, they were baptized to be cleansed of all pagan impurity and to identify with the Jews in being part of the Mosaic Covenant. Native Jews were not baptized before this time. Repentance represented changing one's mind about sin. Repentance was an act of mourning one's sin because it broke God's heart. The result of repentance was changing one's behavior to not do that sin any longer. Jews knew about repentance. But the normal practice for receiving forgiveness of sins came from the shedding of blood through animal sacrifices (Hebrews 9:22).

LESSON 1

8. So what were the people recognizing in their lives when they responded to John's call for repentance and, thus, to be baptized?

9. Read Malachi 4:5-6. What did God promise to the people?

10. Read 2 Kings 1:8 and compare what you read with how John is described in Mark 1:6. What message was John conveying to the people? See also Malachi 3:1; 4:5.

11. In Mark 1:7-8, Mark again answers the question, "Who is Jesus?" What does John say about the one coming?

12. **Heartbreak to Hope:** Why would listening to John's preaching in the wilderness give hope to the people who came to hear him?

Respond to the Lord about what He's shown you today.

DAY THREE STUDY

Ask the Lord Jesus to speak to you through His Word. Tell Him that you are listening.

Read Mark 1:1-13.

13. *Discover the Facts:* Focus on vv. 9-11. A lot of truth is packed into these three verses.

    Where was Jesus (v. 9)?

    What did Jesus see (v. 10)?

    What did God the Father say to God the Son (v. 11)?

14. Jesus never did sin. Why did He come to be baptized? [Review the "Focus on the Meaning" in Day Two.]

15. Read John 1:32-34. What was one purpose for the Spirit descending on Jesus in a visible "dove" form?

> **Scriptural Insight:** While confirming that there is only one true God, believers have worshiped Jesus Christ and have spoken of Him in terms appropriate only of deity from the earliest days of Christianity (first century A.D.). The Holy Spirit is also known as deity. So the only conclusion is that the Bible clearly teaches three Divine Persons, each rightly called God, yet all the one and same God. The doctrine of the *Trinity* (or "Tri-unity," a man-made label) is then a summary of the teachings of the Bible regarding the nature of God. God is one in essence, three in Person. It is an unexplainable reality, part of the mystery of God. All three persons of the Trinity are present at the baptism of Jesus. You can consider this event as Jesus' commissioning for ministry. All three persons are united in the mission set forth for Jesus.

16. Read John 8:29. What does Jesus say about His own goal in life?

17. Did you notice that God the Father told His Son that He was well pleased with Him before Jesus' ministry even began? What does this reveal about God's love for His Son for the 30 years before this day?

18. **Heartbreak to Hope:** Have you had to wait for something for a very long time? Did you think God was being lazy or had forgotten you? Maybe He was preparing the background for answering your prayer as He did during the 30 years before Jesus showed up for all to see. Can you look back now and recognize how God was at work on your behalf or for someone you love?

Respond to the Lord about what He's shown you today.

Day Four Study

Ask the Lord Jesus to speak to you through His Word. Tell Him that you are listening.

Read Mark 1:1-13.

19. According to Mark 1:12-13, what happens next and why?

20. Who helped Jesus (v. 13)?

> **Historical Insight:** Mark mentions Jesus being in the presence of wild animals. Considering his Christian audience in Rome knew of the fights to the death involving humans versus wild animals in the Colosseum, perhaps Mark was showing how Jesus could identify with them in that way too.

21. What else interests you from Mark 1:1-13?

22. *Heartbreak to Hope:* Reflect back on this whole lesson, how did someone experiencing heartbreak, pain, or uncertainty find hope, healing and love?

Respond to the Lord about what He's shown you today.

> **Recommended:** Listen to the podcast "Jesus and the Kingdom of God" after doing this lesson to reinforce what you have learned. Use the following listener guide.

LESSON 1

PODCAST LISTENER GUIDE

Jesus and the Kingdom of God

"The time has come…The kingdom of God has come near. Repent and believe the good news!" (Mark 1:15)

GOD'S KINGDOM BEGAN AT CREATION.

- The whole idea of kingship is God's idea. When we talk about God as king, we are talking about the rule of God Almighty over His entire creation, including all people. *Daniel 4:34*

- God set up a theocratic kingdom at Creation. God was the ultimate ruler. But He chose to give Adam and Eve responsibility as God's servants in God's kingly rule over the creation.

- Because sin separated people from a direct relationship with God, God's rule became a representative rule through delegated authorities. *Genesis 10:8-12; Genesis 17:6; Genesis 35:11; Genesis 49:10; Daniel 5:21; Romans 13:1*

GOD CHOSE ISRAEL TO BE A THEOCRWATIC NATION.

- God set up Israel as a theocratic nation with God as her King. The sacrificial system in the Law temporarily removed sin from the people so God could dwell with them. *Deuteronomy 33:5s*

- Israel was not content with the theocracy and demanded a strong human ruler to be their king. But the king of Israel was still under God's authority.

- Faithful Israelites considered God to be their ultimate King and themselves to be part of His Kingdom, even within the nation of Israel.

THE PROMISED MESSIAH'S ROLE IN GOD'S KINGDOM

- After Saul's failure to honor God, He chose David to be the next king of Israel, a man who loved God and would represent God well as he ruled Israel. Through David, God made a promise to have one of David's descendants to be on Israel's throne forever. *Psalm 2; Psalm 110*

- Messiah as a descendant of David is one whom God had chosen to rule in His name as the official representative of God's rule over His people. The kingdom of God would once again come to earth. The ultimate fulfillment of this promise is in Jesus.

GOD SENT MESSIAH JESUS TO OFFER ENTRANCE INTO HIS KINGDOM.

- At His birth, Jesus came announced as a King, qualifying for the throne of David through both Mary and Joseph. *Luke 1:32-33*

- At the age of 30, Jesus began to proclaim that the Kingdom of God was near and whoever repented from their lack of faith and believed in Him would enter that forever Kingdom.

- For 3 years, Jesus demonstrated that He is God as He delivered men and women from their physical and spiritual ills.

- When Jesus entered Jerusalem on a donkey (Mark 11), the crowds understood that Jesus was presenting Himself as the Messiah, capable of bringing in the Kingdom.

THE KING HAD TO SUFFER FIRST TO DELIVER HIS PEOPLE.

- In Jerusalem, Jesus was rejected as the King—as God's representative to rule in God's place on earth. God's plan was to first deal with sin once and for all so He could have a restored relationship with His creation.

- The Jews of expected the Messiah to redeem Israel by overthrowing the rule of the Romans and establishing an earthly kingdom. But the Messiah would first deliver His people *spiritually*; that is, to redeem them from sin. Later, Jesus the Messiah will deliver His people from their physical enemies, when He sets up His Kingdom on the earth.

GOD'S KINGDOM—JESUS IN HEAVEN

- The time between Jesus' ascension to heaven and His return to earth is called the "until" time (Luke 21:24). Every believer in Jesus Christ for the past 2000 years is part of God's Kingdom, now headquartered in heaven where our King Jesus resides and has all authority over heaven and earth. *Ephesians 1:21-23; Philippians 2:9-11*

GOD'S KINGDOM—JESUS ON EARTH

- The Bible teaches that at the end of a 7-year period commonly called "The Great Tribulation," Jesus Christ will bring His physical Kingdom to Earth for 1000 years with Jerusalem as His capital. *Revelation 1:5; 17:14; 19:16; 20:4*

- In this earthly Kingdom, Jesus Christ will be the supreme political ruler as well as the spiritual leader and object of worship. The government of Christ will be one of absolute authority and power. It will also be one of righteousness and peace. All Christians will have been given resurrection bodies and will participate with Christ in administering His earthly kingdom. *Psalm 2; 72; Isaiah 11; Daniel 7:13 14*

The Kingdom of God is the dynamic rule of God manifested in Christ to destroy His enemies (sin, death, and Satan) and to bring to men the blessings of God's reign. Jesus told His disciples in Matthew 6 that we should pray for His Kingdom to come and for God's will to be done on Earth as it is done in heaven. That will happen after the "until time" in which we now live.

Let Jesus satisfy your heart with hope, healing, and love as you get to know Him and trust Him more each day.

Lesson 2: Friends, Family, and Fast-spreading News

(Mark 1:14-45)

Day One Study

Ask the Lord Jesus to speak to you through His Word. Tell Him that you are listening.

Read Mark 1:13-20.

Between verses 13 and 14, Mark switched from John's work to focus on Jesus' ministry instead. He skipped about a year of Jesus' public ministry in Judea (covered in John chapters 1-4). During that year, Jesus began to gain followers as He proclaimed the nearness of the kingdom of God that the Jews had been wanting for so long.

1. **Discover the Facts:** After John is put into prison, all eyes are now on Jesus.

    Where did Jesus go (v. 14)?

    What message did Jesus proclaim in vv. 14-15?

    Was this different than what John had proclaimed (see Matthew 3:2)?

    How should someone get ready (v. 15)?

    Think About It: Jesus didn't say they needed to get ready for the coming kingdom by gathering their swords, axes, or other weapons. He said they must repent and believe the good news. There's that word "repent" again. To repent means to change your unbelief to belief, to mourn your sins and choose God's way of approaching life.

    Who does Jesus see as He walks by the Sea of Galilee (vv. 16, 19)?

    What does Jesus say to Simon and Andrew (v. 17)?

    What was their responsibility?

Focus on the Meaning: His invitation to all these men was two-fold. 1) To follow Jesus. That phrase literally means, "to come alongside or walk the same road." He was challenging them to be His disciples. Rabbis had disciples. This relationship lasted for months or years. Disciples learn from their "rabbi" and apply what they learn to their lives. 2) Fishers of people—they would be disciple-makers. Fishing is a transferable concept. Their tools and skills for fishing would be transferred to targeting and reaching people in Jesus' plan. He would give them training and opportunities. Plus, hanging out together would foster intimacy in their relationship with Jesus.

What was the response of all 4 men (vv. 18, 20)?

2. Read John 1:35-42. What was Jesus' first interaction with the brothers Simon and Andrew?

Scriptural Insight: We know from Mark 1:20 that James and John were the sons of Zebedee. From the lists of the women near the cross (Matthew 27:56; Mark 15:40 and John 19:25), we can conclude that the mother of Zebedee's children was named Salome and that she was also Mary's (Jesus' mother) sister. That makes her Jesus' aunt, and her sons (James and John) would be Jesus' first cousins. So Jesus knew all 4 of these men before this day recorded in Mark 1.

3. Read Luke 5:4-7. What did Jesus give them so they could follow Him immediately?

Historical Insight: Fishing from the Sea of Galilee was a lucrative business. The lake teemed with big fish so the fishermen were prosperous. Peter, Andrew, James and John made a good living. They would have dried, pickled and preserved their fish, then sold it to merchants who delivered it to other parts of the Roman world by way of Rome's extensive highway system. Zebedee, his sons, and Simon and Andrew were partners in the fishing business. Jesus gave them so much fish that this likely provided resources for their families for months!

The 2009 movie *Julie and Julia* is a great illustration of disciple-making. The move portrays young Julie Powell becoming a disciple of the chef Julia Child through Julia's cookbook, *Mastering the Art of French Cooking*. As a disciple, Julie studies the recipes and follows the procedures. She experiences the joy of cooking and eating delicious food as Julia taught her through the book. Julie got to know Julia Child "personally" though they never met. In a sense, Julie "followed" Julia. Julie didn't keep what she was learning about cooking to herself, though. She wrote a blog, bringing others along with her. Then, she wrote a book that was turned into a movie. Many women bought Julia Child's book and started cooking through it because of Julie's influence. That's disciple-making. While she was following Julia Child as her disciple, Julie Powell was introducing other people to Julia, sharing what she was learning so they could cook that way too. Julie was a follower and a disciple-maker at the same time. That's what Jesus wants from us too—to be followers of Him and disciple-makers for Him at the same time.

4. ***Heartbreak to Hope:*** Christianity is Christ—all about a relationship with Him. It's not a society, an organization, or a set of rules. It's a relationship-based new way to approach life with freedom and joy.

    - Like Peter, Andrew, James and John, have you already made the decision to trust in Christ for your salvation and follow Him?

    - Perhaps you don't have a relationship with Christ and would like to understand what it's all about. This is the "Good News" about Jesus (often called the Gospel message):

    God created you to enjoy a relationship with Himself. Sadly, your sin (the ways you have gone against what God wants for you) has separated you from a holy God and caused spiritual death in you. But God gave His Son, Jesus Christ, who became human, lived a perfect life, died, and was resurrected to pay sin's death penalty. You receive God's gift of forgiveness of your sin by trusting in Jesus as the Son of God who died to take away your sin. At that moment, you receive eternal life and begin a new relationship with Christ. And you gain a new purpose in life, which is to follow Him and enjoy Him forever.

    Are you ready to trust in Jesus Christ now?

Respond to the Lord about what He's shown you today.

Day Two Study

Ask the Lord Jesus to speak to you through His Word. Tell Him that you are listening.

Read Mark 1:21-28.

5. ***Discover the Facts:*** Mark introduced his readers to the teachers of the law (also known as lawyers or scribes). These men were like modern lawyers or seminary professors, proficient in their subject area—in this case, the Mosaic Law. The teachers of the law usually quoted other people. But Jesus taught with His own authority (vv. 22, 27).

    What did Jesus do on the Sabbath (v. 21)?

    How did the people respond (v. 22)?

    Who was in the audience (v. 23)?

    What did "he" say (v. 24)?

    Jesus told the evil spirit to "be quiet," which literally means "be muzzled" (v. 25). How did the demon respond, showing it was still in rebellion (v. 26)?

    How did the watching audience respond (v. 27)?

    Then, what happened (v. 28)?

    > **Scriptural Insight:** The unclean or evil spirit was a demon. Demons were angels created at the beginning of creation. One rebelled against God and took 1/3 of the angels with him (Luke 10:18; Hebrews 12:22; Revelation 12:3-9). We know that rebel leader as Satan, "the accuser." Demons are under him as angels in rebellion against God. They do everything they can to thwart the purpose of God, gaining control over people through deception, counterfeits, fear, manipulation, and torment. It seems that during Jesus' life on earth Satan launched a counter attack through demonic possession of individuals. The evil

spirit identified Jesus correctly. Jesus as the Son of God had the power to destroy them; He was their adversary as the Holy One of God. He defeated the enemy by driving out demons, demonstrating His authority over all the spirit world—the good angels who served Him plus Satan and his demonic forces. Jesus is more powerful than Satan and any demon. Nothing good can come from demons, which may be why Jesus commanded them to be silent about His identity.

6. **Heartbreak to Hope:** What in today's study speaks to your heart?

Respond to the Lord about what He's shown you today.

Day Three Study

Ask the Lord Jesus to speak to you through His Word. Tell Him that you are listening.

Read Mark 1:29-34

7. **Discover the Facts:** We think news travels fast today. But it traveled fast 2000 years ago. From noon to sunset, the word spread that Jesus was in town, and He had healed someone. Answer these questions based on what is in the text.

   Who left the synagogue with Jesus and where did they go (v. 29)?

   What did they find there (v. 30)?

   How did Jesus respond to that news (v. 31)?

   What was her response back to Him?

Who showed up at Peter's door that evening (vv. 32-33)?

Scriptural Insight: In Scripture, a miracle is an act of God that cannot be explained by natural means. God's purpose for miracles in the Bible seems to be three-fold. 1) To authenticate the messenger and, therefore, the message. Jesus' miracles showed that He is God. He has authority. The Kingdom is in His presence. 2) To demonstrate God's compassion for His people. We will repeatedly see how Jesus' miracles certainly did that. 3) To show the power of God. Only God's power can do the things that Jesus did. Jesus is God on earth.

God still heals today, instantly or through enabling the body to heal itself. But He makes no blanket promise to do so during this time in which we live. Where God chooses to allow affliction and trouble to remain in our lives, He promises hope through comfort and through teaching us how to depend on Him. We learn to trust Him with what He chooses to do.

Read Mark 1:35-39.

8. ***Discover the Facts:*** Jesus makes a few intentional choices. See what they are in this passage.

    What did Jesus do the next morning (v. 35)?

    When the disciples found Him, what did they say (v. 37)?

    What was Jesus' plan that fit with His purpose (v. 38)?

    What did he do (v. 39)?

The people of Capernaum would have kept Him there as their in-house healer. Jesus knew His purpose was beyond that. He wanted to get the message out. A relationship with God was more important than just physical healing. He traveled to all the little towns in the region, each about a mile or two apart, and taught in the synagogues. This time of travel probably lasted a couple of months.

LESSON 2

9. ***Heartbreak to Hope:*** If Jesus needed time alone with God and intentionally made that happen, we need it far more. That personal time with God is often called a "quiet time." Read the following quote than answer the questions below it.

> **Think About It:** In her book, "A Practical Guide to Prayer," Dorothy Haskins tells about a noted concert violinist who was asked the secret of her mastery of the instrument. The woman answered the question with two words, "PLANNED NEGLECT." Then she explained, "There were many things that used to demand my time. When I went to my room after breakfast, I made my bed, straightened the room, dusted and did whatever seemed necessary. When I finished my work, I turned to my violin practice. That system prevented me from accomplishing what I should on the violin. So I reversed things. I **deliberately planned to neglect everything else until** my practice period was complete. And that program of planned neglect is the secret of my success."

There are many good things we can choose to do with our day. Unless we discipline ourselves and make a deliberate effort, good things and the tyranny of the urgent rob us of spending time with God in Bible reading and prayer. Reflect on how you spend your day. What do you do or can you do to intentionally withdraw from activity to be alone with God and His Word? What "Planned Neglect" could you practice?

Respond to the Lord about what He's shown you today.

Day Four Study

Ask the Lord Jesus to speak to you through His Word. Tell Him that you are listening.

Read Mark 1:40-45.

10. ***Discover the Facts:*** A man came to Jesus with a great need.

    A man with leprosy came to Jesus and asked what (v. 40)?

    The leper had faith in Jesus' ability to heal him, recognizing God's choice not questioning God's ability. How did Jesus respond to the man (v. 41)?

Focus on the Meaning: In v. 41, "compassion (NIV)" is a better translation than "pity (ESV)." Jesus felt compassion for the man. Compassion means that you are moved with a desire to do something to help. It is not just feeling sorry for someone. How long had it been since someone touched the leper? The Jews were concerned about becoming ceremonially unclean if they touched someone sick. Uncleanness was not sin. But it restricted their interaction with others in the community and their attendance at the synagogue until they were purified through passage of time (a new day) or an offering. Others would be made ceremonially unclean if they touched the leper, but nothing made Jesus unclean.

After being healed, what instructions did Jesus give to the man (vv. 43-44)?

What happened instead (v. 45)?

Scriptural Insight: Why did Jesus tell people not to speak about their healing? It could be for several reasons: 1) Jesus did not want to be considered just a miracle worker, (2) He did not want His teaching ministry hindered by too much publicity being given to His healing miracles, and (3) He did not want His death to come prematurely, i.e., before He had finished His ministry. (*NIV Study Bible 1984 Edition,* note on Matthew 8:4, p. 1453)

11. *Heartbreak to Hope:* Crowds begged for Jesus to do something all the time. It probably felt for Him like it does for us at a sold-out concert or athletic event. If you are a parent or teacher, the crowds were like children who won't leave you alone or who continually pester you about something. Or perhaps this is how you feel at work, constantly surrounded by people with needs. Jesus understands how you feel. He's been there. Do you have confidence in that?

12. *Heartbreak to Hope:* Reflect back on this whole lesson, how did someone experiencing heartbreak, pain, or uncertainty find hope, healing and love?

Respond to the Lord about what He's shown you today.

Recommended: Listen to the podcast "Jesus Satisfies Your Heart with Hope" after doing this lesson to reinforce what you have learned. Use the following listener guide.

LESSON 2

PODCAST LISTENER GUIDE

Jesus Satisfies Your Heart with Hope

WE ALL NEED HOPE.

Biblical hope is the confident expectation that God will fulfill His promises to you because your hope is based on the character and faithfulness of God.

HOPE THROUGH HEALING

"Praise the Lord, O my soul, and forget not all His benefits—who forgives all your sins and heals all your diseases." (Psalm 103:2)

Why did Jesus perform so many miracles?

- Miracles authenticate the message and the messenger. Jesus' miracles demonstrated that He is God and that His message has authority.

- Jesus demonstrated God's compassion for His people in healing their diseases.

- Jesus showed that He has power beyond that of an ordinary man. The laws of the natural world, which He created, were not boundaries for Him.

- The miracles were also evidence that Jesus was the fulfillment of prophecy concerning the Messiah.

- Jesus showed that He was God on earth.

How does God still heal today?

- God still performs miracles today though we may not see them as often as we'd like. Miracles are initiated by God. People are the miracle conduits.

- Miracles still authenticate the message and the messenger. For someone claiming to do miraculous things, always make sure their message exalts Jesus as the **only** way to God, that the Bible is their **only** authority, and that forgiveness of sins is found **only** through Jesus Christ. Then, you can be confident that you are seeing the genuine works of God.

- Remember that the greatest miracle of all is what God does to change a human heart from the inside out and redeem a lost life. He is doing that in abundance everywhere.

- In Psalm 103, the phrase "heals all your diseases" could also refer to God enabling the human body to heal itself.

- Jesus has the right to choose what He brings into our lives. We will see throughout Mark that He tells us to stop being afraid, to keep on believing, and to hold onto hope.

HOPE THROUGH COMFORT WHEN HEALING IS DELAYED

"Praise be to the God and Father of our Lord Jesus Christ, the Father of compassion and the God of all comfort, who comforts us in all our troubles," (2 Corinthians 1:3)

- The promise is that our God comforts us in ALL our troubles, including those that happen to us like chronic illness as well as those we cause because of wrong choices we make.

- God chose not to heal Paul's physical ailment. Paul's response was to rejoice in his weakness so that Christ's power would be on him. Being able to rejoice in your weakness frees you from bondage to it and moves you in the direction that will give you hope. 2 Corinthians 12:9

- Through any life challenge, including physical debilitation, God wants us to learn to depend more on God and His great power and to rely less on ourselves. Sometimes we want to just quit. It's God's power in us that makes us strong during those times. In His strength, we receive hope through comfort.

"There were always only two answers to your prayers—either she was going to be healed or she was going to be healed. Either she was going to live, or she was going to live. Either she was going to be with family, or she was going to be with family. Either she was going to be well taken care of, or she was going to be well taken care of....The two answers to your prayer are yes and yes. Because victory belongs to Jesus." (Jonathan Evans)

- We have a big God. Yet, God may not choose to rescue you from everything that is threatening you or from poor decisions made by you or someone close to you. You may face what seem like insurmountable circumstances in your life. You may have to give up something that gives you security. You may be waiting for God to answer a desperate prayer. Are you willing to accept the yes He wants to give?

- You may feel that God isn't noticing your pain. He knows. He chooses what will make you more like the Lord Jesus Christ. And suffering is an important instrument in His hands much as you may hate it.

- In your pain, you can say to Him, "I am your daughter, Lord. Help me to deal with this situation through your power. Please give me your hope and comfort."

- Remember that God is good all the time. You can trust His goodness in whatever He chooses to do in your life. Trouble is part of human life. Christians who are loved by God will suffer some troubles in this world, but **Jesus is Your comforter** when you hurt.

Let Jesus satisfy your heart with hope, healing, and love as you get to know Him and trust Him more each day.

Lesson 3: Forgiving, Calling, Claiming, & Appointing

(Mark 2:1-3:19)

Jesus knew our greatest need. It wasn't health or wealth. It was removal of the sin barrier between us and God. The needs of the heart trump the physical needs. He presents this to the people in His interaction with those who seem to ignore this truth or think they can't be worthy in God's sight.

DAY ONE STUDY

Ask the Lord Jesus to speak to you through His Word. Tell Him that you are listening.

Read Mark 2:1-12.

> **Historical Insight:** Capernaum was a fairly large town with about 1500 residents and the major center of trade and commerce in Galilee. The international trade route from Egypt through Palestine to Syria and Mesopotamia passed nearby. Caravans came through with travelers and merchants from many nations and stations of life—not only Jews but non-Jews (also called Gentiles). It was also a tax collecting center for the Romans. Travelers and merchants had to stop and pay a tax on their way through town. Fishermen and farmers had to pay a tax when they sent out their products. So a lot of tax collectors were headquartered in Capernaum—like Levi in Mark 2. Roman soldiers were stationed there to keep peace at this busy intersection.
> The climate was so good that the locals thought of Capernaum as a "paradise." Palm trees grew along the boulevards. Fruits and vegetables multiplied so the farmers were prosperous as were the fishermen. Nearly everyone lived on the same level economically. Jesus adopted Capernaum as His hometown and the center of His ministry in Galilee. Five of His 12 disciples came from there. It was an ideal place for Jesus to spread out His message. And the inhabitants of Capernaum had many opportunities to see and hear Jesus.

1. **Discover the Facts:** It is generally thought that Peter's house in Capernaum was Jesus' home base. Since Peter was married (Mark 1:30; 1 Corinthians 9:5), see what is happening here through the eyes of his wife (Mrs. Peter). The people heard that Jesus had come home. Picture crowds inside and outside the house.

   What is Jesus doing in the crowded house (v. 2)?

   What happens next (vv. 3-4)?

   What does Jesus see and say (v. 5)?

Some religious lawyers were also present and watching. What were they thinking to themselves (v. 7)?

What does Jesus know about them and say to them (vv. 8-9)?

Why does He then heal the man (vv. 10-11)?

What happens next (v. 12)?

> **Historical Insight:** The Pharisees were an influential group of ~6000 men whose goal for about 150 years was that Israel would stay true to Judaism and never go back to idolatry. So they emphasized keeping every bit of the law of Moses plus 100s of man-made laws. Since the Pharisees found that other Jews were not careful enough keeping those laws, they looked on other people as tainted by sin and, therefore, to be avoided. By Jesus' day, they had become so self-satisfied with their law-keeping that they were hard-hearted to the things of God and His people. The "teachers of the law" (also called "scribes" or "lawyers") were like today's seminary professors since many of them taught in the Jerusalem seminary.

2. What did the 4 men think their friend's most important need was? How do you know?

3. What did Jesus think was the man's most important need? How do you know?

> **Scriptural Insight:** This is an illustration of the difference between real needs and felt needs. Whereas the paralyzed man's felt need was his need to walk again, his real need was to remove the barrier of sin that separated him from God. In Jesus' mind, the man's real need trumped his physical needs. Jesus took care of his real need first then his felt need. We see him doing this by teaching crowds of people everywhere He went about a relationship with God even while healing those who were sick.

LESSON 3

4. What is missing in the religious leaders' attitude toward the paralyzed man?

> **Think About It:** The Jews in bondage to Rome longed for the Kingdom. Jesus offered them the Kingdom and freedom from their bondage to sin. Many rejected it.

5. ***Heartbreak to Hope:*** The Pharisees and teachers of the law are always watching Jesus, always finding fault with Him. How do you feel about someone who always finds fault with you? Jesus gets it. He dealt with it every day.

Read Mark 2:13-17 and Luke 5:27-32.

> **Historical Insight:** Tax collectors sat at a tollbooth along the highways collecting Roman taxes on toll roads and customs on merchandise. They were considered greedy, on a get-rich-quick path to success since they could exact a surcharge on people, charging up to 4 times the tax fee itself. Because they were in collusion with the Romans, they were hated by most Jews as cheats and traitors. The tax collectors and their wives were not permitted to attend the synagogue. So they formed their own social group. As to skills, tax collectors were educated men who could write in Hebrew, Latin, and Greek. They carried an inkwell and paper with them to use for record keeping. The fact that Levi has two names—Levi Matthew—speaks to his wealth and prominence in the community. You will see throughout the gospels that tax collectors were drawn to Jesus.

6. ***Discover the Facts:*** Jesus calls another man to become His disciple—Levi, whom we know better as Matthew, the writer of the gospel by that name.

   While Jesus is again teaching a large crowd, whom does He invite to follow Him (v. 14)?

   When Jesus says, "Follow me," how does Levi respond (v. 14)?

> **Think About It:** Jesus knew Levi's longing heart and offered hope by saying 2 words, "Follow me." If there was a Mrs. Levi, she shared in her husband's disgrace. When Jesus got a hold of her husband, it would affect her life as well.

Later, Jesus is invited to a dinner in Levi's house. Who is there (v. 15)? See also Luke 5:29.

When the religious lawyers showed up outside to listen and watch, what did they see Jesus doing (v. 16)?

When asked why He was eating with tax collectors and sinners, what is Jesus' answer to them (v. 17)? See also Matthew 9:13.

>   **Focus on the Meaning:** Sinners were the really bad people such as money-changers, thieves and prostitutes. They were considered scum like the tax collectors but from a lower class. According to the Pharisees' teaching, God's mercy extended only to those who kept the Law (including their laws). But what is mercy? It is being pardoned and not getting the judgment or punishment we deserve. Forgiveness of sins is mercy. Jesus offered mercy to every tax collector and sinner. Levi said yes to the offer and probably left 10 times more income to follow Jesus than the fishermen did. Levi is known more by his other name Matthew (beloved of God) which speaks of his new identity. He also got a new way to use his writing skills. The Gospel of Matthew is the longest gospel and contains more of Jesus' sermons than any other. In it, he refers to himself as "Matthew, the tax collector"—what he is now (beloved) and how he was known before Jesus came into his life.

7. Read Luke 3:12-13. Tax collectors were drawn to John the Baptist's preaching and came to be baptized. What did he tell them?

8. *Heartbreak to Hope:* The paralyzed man was in need. But so was healthy, wealthy Levi.
   - Do you know someone like that who is smart and seemingly doing well in life but hopeless? Someone who is desperately in need of God's mercy right now? What about that woman next door or sitting in that office? What can you tell her about your own acceptance of Jesus' offer of mercy to you that would give them hope?

   - Are you the one needing God's mercy right now? Will you accept Jesus' offer of mercy and forgiveness so your life can be changed by Jesus like Matthew's life was changed?

- Perhaps your own "house neighbors" need the Jesus living in you to extend mercy to them, the kind of mercy you've already received from Him. Ask Jesus to help you do this.

Respond to the Lord about what He's shown you today.

Day Two Study

Ask the Lord Jesus to speak to you through His Word. Tell Him that you are listening.

Read Mark 2:18-22.

> **Scriptural Insight:** Fasting is a voluntary abstinence from food and/or drink as an expression of religious devotion. In the Old Testament, God prescribed one yearly fast for all Jews on the Day of Atonement as an act of repentance and mourning over sin. By the time of the New Testament, some Jews practiced personal "fasting" (for example, Anna in Luke 2:37). Jesus did not by practice or by teaching stress fasting. The Pharisees promoted voluntary fasts for their disciples twice a week (on Mondays and Thursdays) as an act of piety. The feast in Levi's house may have occurred on one of those days. Jesus' parable referred to the Jewish custom exempting the friends of the bridegroom from certain religious obligations such as the weekly fasts. God was doing something new and different. It was the time for celebrating, not mourning, because the long-awaited Kingdom was here. After Pentecost, Jewish Christians continued to fast, but there is no record of Gentile Christians doing so.

9. ***Discover the Facts***: This is a curious passage. The Pharisees are continually challenging Jesus' practices and comparing those to what they consider acceptable.

   What oppositional question do they ask (v. 18)?

   How does Jesus answer them in vv. 19-20?

   What does He say about adding new things to old forms (vv. 21-22)?

   > **Think About It:** As Christians, we operate under grace and are free to fast or not to fast as we feel led by the Spirit of God to do so. Any time you feel coerced by others to fast, go to

the Lord and ask Him, "Is this what you want me to do?" The Lord is pleased with whatever you give Him, as long as it is His idea and His power and not something you do in your own flesh (in your own power without relying on Him). (Sue Bohlin, Probe Ministries)

Read Mark 2:23-28.

10. ***Discover the Facts:*** Does it seem to you like the Pharisees are stalking Jesus? Here they are again with another oppositional question.

    One Sabbath, what was Jesus doing (v. 23)?

    What is the question asked by the Pharisees this time (v. 24)?

    How does Jesus answer them (vv. 25-26)?

    Then, what does He teach about the purpose of the Sabbath (v. 27)?

    What claim does He make for Himself (v. 28)?

11. It was according to the Pharisees that Jesus' actions were unlawful, not according to God. Anyone can feed themselves on the Sabbath. The restriction to working on the Sabbath was for work that led to harvesting a crop to sell. Were Jesus and His disciples doing this?

Respond to the Lord about what He's shown you today.

Day Three Study

Ask the Lord Jesus to speak to you through His Word. Tell Him that you are listening.

Read Mark 3:1-6.

> **Historical Insight:** According to Dr. Paul Brand, the late world-renowned leprosy physician, the best example in the Bible of a person with Hansen's disease is the man with the withered hand in Mark 3:5. He likely suffered from tuberculoid leprosy. (*Answers Magazine*, Vol. 2 No. 3, "Biblical Leprosy: Shedding Light on the Disease that Shuns," p. 78)

12. **Discover the Facts:** Thinking of what is lawful to do on the Sabbath in their minds (2:24), Jesus' opposition closely watched Him to see what He would do in the synagogue.

    What is the situation (vv. 1-2)?

    What did Jesus say anyway (v. 3)?

    What question does Jesus ask to counter their illogical thinking (v. 4)?

    > **Think About It:** The Pharisees believed in Jesus' power to perform miracles. The question was not "Could He?" but "Would He?" Jewish tradition prescribed that aid could be given the sick on the Sabbath only when the person's life was threatened, which obviously was not the case here. (*NIV Study Bible 1984 Edition*, note on Mark 3:2, p. 1497)

    What did He recognize in them, and how did He feel about that (v. 5)?

    What happens next (v. 5)?

    What is the response of the opposition to Jesus now (v. 6)?

    > **Historical Insight:** The Herodians were influential Jews who supported Rome. Normally, the Pharisees would have avoided them in every possible situation. But their hatred of Jesus is so strong that they plot to kill Him. Now, who is really breaking the Law of Moses? The legalists plotted to break the Law to kill Jesus.

Jesus had a normal human emotional response of anger and distress against the stubborn hearts of the religious people who think they have it "right" and are not teachable. Their hard hearts angered and saddened our Lord. The Jewish people looked up to these religious leaders and were being led away from God, not toward Him, by their influence.

13. ***Heartbreak to Hope:*** Do you also feel anger and distress against hard-hearted people in your life? Jesus understands exactly how you feel. He didn't stop teaching truth to those who were in opposition to Him or whose hearts seemed so uncompassionate towards the hurting. He did the right thing. He can help you do the right thing, also. Just ask for it.

Read Mark 3:7-12.

14. ***Discover the Facts:*** More crowds, more teaching, and more demonstrations of God's power present in Jesus ...

What did Jesus do (v. 7)?

What kept Him from getting away with His disciples (vv. 8-9)?

What did He use to help Him stay focused on His priority of teaching the crowd (vv. 10-11; 4:1)?

What interaction did Jesus have with the evil spirits (vv. 11-12)?

15. ***Heartbreak to Hope:*** What in today's lesson speaks to your heart?

Respond to the Lord about what He's shown you today.

LESSON 3

Day Four Study

Ask the Lord Jesus to speak to you through His Word. Tell Him that you are listening.

Read Mark 3:13-19 and Luke 6:12-16.

16. ***Discover the Facts***: Jesus needed to make a big decision. He would choose some of His many followers (disciples) to be appointed for special service.

    What did He do before this moment (Luke 6:12-13)?

    Where did Jesus go to call together those He wanted (v. 13)?

    How many did He appoint and designate "apostles" (v. 14)?

    What would be their three-fold purpose (vv. 14-15)?

17. List those He chose plus what is said about them. Note: when comparing the lists in Matthew 10:2-4 and Luke 6:14-16 with what is here in Mark, some men were known by two names (Bartholomew was also Nathaniel; Thaddeus was also called Judas son of James).

    From the Greek: The word translated "apostle" means "delegate, one sent with a special commission."

18. Why would it be good to have these 12 dedicated Apostles? Consider all the various aspects of being with Jesus.

37

19. ***Heartbreak to Hope:*** Though we are not called to be "Apostles," we are called by Jesus to be with Him. We are with Him continually because His Spirit lives in us. But we can be with Him like the Apostles were through what He chose to have His Apostles record for us—now the New Testament writings. When you spend time reading a portion of the New Testament, you are with Jesus so He can teach you and send you out to tell others what you learned from Him. When is your daily designated time to be with Jesus?

20. ***Heartbreak to Hope:*** Reflect back on this whole lesson, how did someone experiencing heartbreak, pain, or uncertainty find hope, healing and love?

Respond to the Lord about what He's shown you today.

Recommended: Listen to the podcast "Walking Home with Jesus" after doing this lesson to reinforce what you have learned. Use the following listener guide.

LESSON 3

PODCAST LISTENER GUIDE

Walking Home with Jesus

Home is where you live—where you do life together with family and friends. Jesus made Himself at home among His new neighbors. And He does the same thing with us. *Mark 2:1; John 14:23*

ENJOYING JESUS' PRESENCE AT HOME (PETER'S HOUSE)

- Scholars and tradition strongly hold that Peter's house became "the house of Jesus" whenever Jesus was in Capernaum.

- In that house were Peter and Andrew, plus Peter's wife—let's call her Mrs. Peter—and Mrs. Peter's mother (Mark 1:30) and probably a few children.

- What do you think it was like for Mrs. Peter to experience Jesus' presence in her home? Of course, there were the fun things like great conversation around the dinner table! What about how He healed her mom? That's answered prayer, isn't it? Jesus not only ate meals that she prepared, He also befriended her husband and discipled him to be a more mature man. And she got to learn from Him herself as He taught in her home.

To enjoy Jesus' presence in your home means to accept it as an absolute fact.

- When you and I hear the good news of Christ and put our faith in Him, the Holy Spirit, who's called the Spirit of Christ, comes to live inside of you and me. We become united with Jesus Christ—one with Him in Spirit. Inside or outside our house, He is with us.

- Sometimes life was a bit challenging for Mrs. Peter with Jesus in her house. Both friends and not-so-nice snobs were ever present.

To enjoy Jesus' presence in your home means giving Him permission to make it His own.

- Whenever Jesus was in Capernaum, He and his disciples probably stayed in Mrs. Peter's house. That meant feeding a bunch more men besides her own. Later, a church met in her home.

- When we go to wherever it is that we live, we walk in that door with our Lord. He wants us to give Him permission to make it His own.

THE NEIGHBORS ENJOYING JESUS' PRESENCE (LEVI'S HOUSE)

- Levi was on a "get rich quick" path of life as a tax collector for the Romans. He was educated, could write in Hebrew, Latin, and Greek, and always carried an inkwell at his waist with some paper for making notes.

- Tax collectors were so despised that they were not allowed to attend synagogue or to testify in court. Healthy, wealthy Levi was a desperate man. Jesus invited him to be a disciple then Jesus walked home with His new neighbor, Levi.

Jesus' presence brings a life change.

- Levi celebrated his new relationship with Jesus by throwing a big party and inviting guys from the office. Jesus came with His disciples and those who followed Him.

- Levi and his wife and friends needed God's mercy just like we do. Mercy is God's amnesty. It's being pardoned and not getting the judgment or punishment we deserve.

- We are supposed to allow Jesus to use His presence in our lives and homes to reach those who are in need of God's mercy.

And Jesus' presence brings new purpose.

- Levi became known by another name, Matthew, meaning, "beloved of God." And Matthew had a new way to use his skills as he wrote the gospel of Matthew.

- Mercy is what Levi and his wife and his friends needed. Jesus offered it to them all—right there in Mrs. Levi's home.

HOMES ARE CENTRAL TO JESUS' MINISTRY ON EARTH.

- In homes, Jesus taught and had discussions with His disciples. He ate with those who loved Him as well as with those who were skeptical of Him. In homes, women sat at His feet, listening to Him teach and tearfully pouring out their hearts to Him.

- Jesus often told people to go home. He basically said, "Go to the ones with whom you have a relationship and introduce me to them."

    "Relationships determine what we believe. We are talked into talking; we are loved into loving; we are related into believing." (Josh McDowell, Dallas Theological Seminary Commencement, May 2005)

You can enjoy Jesus' presence in your life and in your home.

Let Jesus satisfy your heart with hope, healing, and love as you get to know Him and trust Him more each day.

Lesson 4: Blasphemy, Parables, and a Stormy Night

(Mark 3:20-4:41)

DAY ONE STUDY

Ask the Lord Jesus to speak to you through His Word. Tell Him that you are listening.

Read Mark 3:20-35 and Matthew 12:22-24.

1. *Discover the Facts:* This section is written in "sandwich" form. Verses 20-21 and verses 31-35 are like two slices of bread with verses 22-30 as the filling between them. It was a common format for writing at the time called a "chiasm." Mark used this format 5 times in his book. Appropriately, this incident took place at mealtime.

   When Jesus entered the house, what did he experience (v. 20)?

   Who heard about this, and what did they decide to do (v. 21)?

   Think About It: Jesus experienced family pressure for Him to rest and stop the craziness. Their intentions were good in that they cared about Him. But they misread the work He was doing. Has this ever happened to you?

   The religious lawyers declared that Jesus was driving out demons with the help of Satan (the prince of demons). How did Jesus explain that their charge is illogical (vv. 23-27)?

   Jesus' mother and brothers arrived. In response to their summons, what did Jesus say that probably shocked the people (vv. 33-34)?

   What is the dividing line (v. 35)?

Jesus hit back hard at the hard-hearted teachers of the law. This discussion of blasphemy has often been misunderstood and wrongly taught. Blasphemy means to slander God or give credit to something else that belongs to Him.

2. Let's look first at the truth of what Jesus said in the context in which He said it. We learn from Matthew that Jesus had just healed a demon-possessed man. What is the real accusation against Jesus by those who are opposing Him (vv. 22, 30)?

3. In verse 28, Jesus declared that people can be forgiven all their sins and every slander they utter. What cannot be forgiven (v. 29)?

> **Focus on the Meaning:** "I tell you the truth" is a statement that says to the listener, "Pay attention. This is very important." It's almost like an oath. Mark records Jesus using this phrase 13 times. It denotes that Jesus was speaking out of His own authority.

4. Let's define blasphemy of the Holy Spirit. Read John 16:8-9 and the definition below to answer the next question.

> **Focus on the Meaning:** Blasphemy against the Holy Spirit is this: "The malicious resistance against the Holy Spirit's converting power after one is shown that Jesus is the Christ." It is like a line in the sand. John 16:8-9 describes the Holy Spirit's role in conversion and the willful unbelief of those who resist Him.

In what ways are the lawyers committing blasphemy against the Holy Spirit? Derive your answer from the verses in Matthew and Mark that you read today.

> **Think About It:** They know the truth and are still choosing against God and are slandering God in the process! He's doing the miracles. Demons don't heal people; God does. Who has been getting all the praise for the healings as they happened so far? God has. Aren't they even listening?

5. *Heartbreak to Hope:* This reference to "family" is a foretaste of the Church. Every believer is adopted into God's family by faith in Jesus. Doing God's will by responding to Jesus makes you "family." Your personal response to Jesus is not dependent on your birth and rearing. The underlying question Jesus is asking the crowd is this, "Will you follow Me more than the influence of your immediate family?" How will you answer that question?

Respond to the Lord about what He's shown you today.

Day Two Study

Ask the Lord Jesus to speak to you through His Word. Tell Him that you are listening.

Read Mark 4:1-20.

Why did Jesus teach with parables? Parables are sermon illustrations usually taken from everyday life or common experiences. They generally teach one main point so not every detail has significance. Some do have more than one application. Those on the outside of Jesus' circle of followers understood the parables, which formed a dividing line between those who were in opposition or just curious and those who were committed to Jesus. Even the unreceptive could remember the parable. If their hearts responded, they could understand its meaning. His followers got the more direct teaching.

6. *Discover the Facts:* This is a well-known parable. Look at it with fresh eyes by answering these questions:

    Describe the setting (v. 1).

    Where did the farmer scatter his seed (vv. 3-8)?

    What happened to the seed in each type of soil?

    What did Jesus say in v. 9?

What did the Twelve ask Him (v. 10)?

Jesus says the listeners have two choices in vv. 11-12. What are they?

> **Focus on the Meaning**: A secret or mystery (vv. 10, 12) in the Bible is something previously unknown but now being revealed. See Deuteronomy 29:29. A lot of things are revealed in the New Testament that were not known or understood in the Old Testament. Jesus drew a distinction between those who accepted His teaching, such as the Twelve, and those who rejected it, such as the [lawyers] and Pharisees. God was giving those who welcomed Jesus' teaching new revelation about the coming messianic kingdom. He was withholding that revelation from those who rejected Him. (*Dr. Constable's Notes on Mark 2017 Edition*, p. 69)

What does the seed represent (v. 14)?

What does the hard path represent (v. 15)?

What do the rocky places represent (vv. 16-17)

What do the thorny places represent (vv. 18-19)?

What does the good soil represent (v. 20)?

> **Focus on the Meaning:** Most commentaries present this "Parable of the Sower" as being about fruitfulness and teachability in response to God. The main point is this: How will you respond to the Word of God sown in you? Truth must be acted upon. Fruitfulness is the result.

7. What are ears to hear (v. 9)? Did the disciples have ears to hear? How do you know?

8. *Heartbreak to Hope:* Where does the soil of your heart fit in this parable? Are you teachable? Are you acting upon the truth you are taught? What evidence of fruitfulness of the Word of God is there in your life? Acting upon the truth of God's Word will bring you hope in those places where you might be experiencing heartbreak or pain.

Respond to the Lord about what He's shown you today.

Day Three Study

Ask the Lord Jesus to speak to you through His Word. Tell Him that you are listening.

Read Mark 4:21-34.

Instead of looking at these parables in detail, you will be discerning what you think is the main idea that Jesus was illustrating with each parable and why you decided that.

9. Focus on vv. 21-25. Note: "Hidden" refers back to "secret / mystery" in v. 11.

    - The main idea of this parable is what?

    - Why did you choose that?

10. Focus on vv. 26-29.

    - The main idea of this parable is what?

    - Why did you choose that?

11. Focus on vv. 30-32.

    - The main idea of this parable is what?

    - Why did you choose that?

12. Focus on vv. 33-34:

    - What did Jesus give to His audience?

    - What did He do for His disciples (the Twelve)? See also v. 11.

    Think About It: If you are a parent or teacher, you can identify with Jesus in discipling children. In a sense, Jesus was discipling His "children" (v. 34) in a way that is very similar to a parent or teacher discipling her children or students.

13. **Heartbreak to Hope:** Jesus mentioned a lamp in v. 21. Lamps give out light. Believers bear the light of the truth about Jesus. We are the walking, talking, visible representatives of the invisible God. As you let His light shine through you, who gets to see and enjoy the light?

Respond to the Lord about what He's shown you today.

Day Four Study

Ask the Lord Jesus to speak to you through His Word. Tell Him that you are listening.

Read Mark 4:35-41.

> **Historical Insight:** Situated in a basin surrounded by mountains, the Sea of Galilee is particularly susceptible to sudden, violent storms. Cool air from the Mediterranean is drawn down through the narrow mountain passes and clashes with the hot, humid air lying over the lake. (*NIV Study Bible 1984 Edition,* note on Mark 4:37, p. 1501)

14. **Discover the Facts:** Have you been in a terrifying rainstorm while in a boat or driving? You will certainly be able to identify with the disciples.

    After teaching all day, Jesus suggested to His disciples that they go to the other side of the lake. So they got into the boat. Who traveled with them (v. 36)?

    What happened while they were in the boat (v. 37)?

    Where is Jesus and why (v. 38)?

    > **Think About It:** When you are so tired you can't even stand up straight, Jesus has been there. He understands exhaustion. You can trust Him to help you and love you through it.

    What do the disciples do and say (v. 38)?

    What did Jesus say to the storm (v. 39)? Note: it's the same thing that He said in Mark 1:25.

    What two questions did He ask of His disciples (v. 40)?

    > **Think About It:** Jesus wasn't worried about Himself or the disciples. God wasn't worried about His Son. He was letting them all go through the storm, letting them struggle. The disciples were worried, though. Did they pray? Or did they just panic? Their question was basically, "Do you care about us?" How often have you asked that same question when you have to struggle through something that is painful, uncomfortable, or fearful?

15. From their response in v. 41, what new appreciation did the disciples have for their "rabbi?"

The question Jesus asked the disciples was directed at their fear. The word He used in v. 40 means "cringing in fear, panic, timid." It never is used positively.

Fear is a normal human emotion designed by God to alert us to danger so we will take action against it. Yet fear can take root in us and cause us to give way to panic and hysteria. Jesus knows this about us. When we are afraid, Jesus wants us to trust Him and not give way to fear. Learning to do so is our walk from fear to faith.

Whenever you are gripped by fear, here are four truths you can apply to any situation. Say these truths to yourself over and over to cement them in your mind:

- ✓ God loves me.
- ✓ God knows what is going on in my life.
- ✓ God can do something about it.
- ✓ I can trust God's goodness in what He chooses to do.

That last truth is the hard part. God is good and what He does is always good (Psalm 119:68). During our time of trusting Him, a loving God will say "no" to some things and "yes" to others. Our choice is to trust His goodness in whatever He chooses to do.

16. **Heartbreak to Hope:** What are the main things that strike fear in your heart? Do you have any specific phobias? Pick one thing that is causing you fear today. Apply the four truths above to that situation. Spend about 5 minutes trusting Jesus with that specific fear in your heart. Just mentally hand it to Him. Then, write it on a card and ask someone in your group (or a trusted friend) to pray for you all week long. Find "Whom Shall I Fear?" by Chris Tomlin on YouTube.com and sing along.

17. **Heartbreak to Hope:** Reflect back on this whole lesson, how did someone experiencing heartbreak, pain, or uncertainty find hope, healing and love?

Respond to the Lord about what He's shown you today.

Recommended: Listen to the podcast "Applying Faith to Fear" after doing this lesson to reinforce what you have learned. Use the following listener guide.

LESSON 4

PODCAST LISTENER GUIDE

Applying Faith to Fear

The Bible teaches that we can face life's realities with courage and peace by entrusting ourselves and our loved ones to a God who loves us dearly.

STORMS OF LIFE HIT.

- In Mark chapter 5, the disciples found themselves in the middle of a fierce storm and got afraid. Jesus asked them why they were cringing in fear and why they didn't believe what He already told them about getting to the other side of the lake.

- Storms of life hit every day to even the most faithful Christians. Every one of us must deal with disappointments, problems, and tragedies in life.

- Fear is a normal human emotion designed by God to alert us to the presence of danger so that we will take action against it. We are supposed to act on it by either fleeing from the danger or facing it head on. Fear is a gift of God.

- Where we get into trouble is when we let our imaginations run wild, give in to despair, and doubt God's goodness. That pessimism comes from our view of trouble.

THE FIRST VIEW IS THE PAGAN, NON-BIBLICAL VIEW OF TROUBLE. IT'S THE WORLD'S VIEW.

- It says that when things go well, the gods are happy with us. When things go wrong, the gods are angry with us. So the goal of life is to stay on the good side of the gods so bad things won't happen.

- Christians can get caught up into this kind of thinking when we try to interpret events, especially tragedies, as *signs* of God's anger or punishment. Don't do it.

- When the disciples asked if Jesus even cared if they drowned, they doubted His love and goodness.

THE GODLY, BIBLICAL VIEW OF TROUBLE

- **Fact #1: We live in a fallen, evil, cursed world.** We are in the last days of this broken old creation which will not get fixed until Jesus returns. In that until time, while we are waiting, you and I have the life of the new creation on the inside through the Holy Spirit. But at the same time, we are living in a body and world of the old, fallen creation.

- **Fact #2: God has chosen from the beginning to give all humans the freedom to act.** Some trouble comes from our own idiotic behavior. We make bad decisions then have to deal with the consequences. They may be hard, but God lets us experience consequences to show us why we need Him more and how ugly our sin really is.

- **Fact #3: We have an enemy named Satan who is real and has influence on our natural world and the people in it.** The devil entices people to rebel against God, and he can cause bad things to happen.

- **Fact #4: Our God is great and powerful and will one day fix this broken world.** That is a promise to us. It will happen in our future.

- Our choice is not whether we will have trouble, but *what kind of* **preparation** *we'll make* and *what* **response** *we'll choose* in facing life's realities when they hit us.

- The preparation is filling your mind with truth from God's Word. That's believing that God is good all the time and that He loves you plus other truths clearly stated in Scripture.

A PROCESS TO APPLY FAITH TO ANY FEAR

1. **Confront it:** What fears do you have right now? Think about them. The worst ones, the real ones, and the imaginary ones.

2. **Ask about each one:** What is my worst-case scenario? Consider just one of those fears. What is the worst that could happen? Think realistically.

3. **Consider this:** If the worst I can imagine happens, could I handle it through the presence and power of Jesus Christ? As a believer, you have the power of the One who created the universe living inside of you. Can He help you get through anything? Yes!

4. **Remember** these four truths and speak them to yourself:
   - *God loves you. John 16:27; Romans 5:5, Ephesians 5:1*
   - *God knows what is going on in your life. Matthew 6:31-32; Psalm 139:1-10*
   - *God can do something about it. Genesis 18:14; Luke 1:37; Mark 10:27*
   - *You can trust His goodness in whatever He chooses to do. Psalm 119:68; Proverbs 3:5*

5. **Pray:** Prayer is simply talking to God about anything and everything. Thank the Lord for His presence and His goodness. Ask Him for the courage and peace to ride out the storm.

6. **Live life securely in Him:** Take common sense precautions. Be wise in the world. Trust God to show you what to do and to give you strength when you are weak.

Let Jesus satisfy your heart with hope, healing, and love as you get to know Him and trust Him more each day.

Lesson 5: Desperation, Deliverance, and Deli on Command

(Mark 5:1-6:56)

DAY ONE STUDY

Ask the Lord Jesus to speak to you through His Word. Tell Him that you are listening.

Read Mark 5:1-20.

> **Historical Insight:** Mark and Luke called this area "the country of the Gerasenes," but Matthew called it the country of the Gadarenes. This incident apparently happened somewhere on the southeast coast of the [Sea of Galilee]. About a mile south of Gersa, there is a fairly steep slope within forty yards from the shore. And about two miles from there, cavern tombs are found which appear to have been used for dwellings. (*Dr. Constable's Notes on Mark 2017 Edition*, pp. 79-80)

1. ***Discover the Facts:*** Jesus headed over to the region of the Gerasenes which was Gentile territory. He encountered someone there who desperately needed Him.

    What do we know about the man (vv. 2-5)?

    What did the man do and say when he saw Jesus and heard what Jesus said (vv. 6-8)?

    The demons in the man begged Jesus not to send them out of the area. They asked Him to allow them to go inside the pigs. The pigs rushed down into the water and drowned (vv. 9-13). When the people heard the news and came to see what happened, what did they see (v. 15)?

    How did the people respond to this "miracle" (vv. 15-17)?

    What was the healed man's response (v. 18)?

    What did Jesus tell him to do (v. 19)?

What did the healed man do (v. 20)?

> **Focus on the Meaning:** Evidently the demons requested permission to enter the swine so they could destroy them. Jesus' permission resulted in everyone seeing the great destructive power and number of the demons, and that the man had experienced an amazing deliverance. Only Mark recorded the number of swine ("about 2,000"). As usual, Mark drew attention to Jesus' awesome power. (*Dr. Constable's Notes on Mark 2017 Edition*, p. 81)

2. Notice the slander the demons made against Jesus in verse 7. Demons are deceivers. Who was really torturing whom in this story?

> **Focus on the Meaning:** When the demons said that they were called "legion, for we are many," they were declaring they represented the many powers opposed to Jesus who were in rebellion against God. ... This story emphasizes the man's pathetic condition as well as the purpose of demonic possession—to torment and destroy the divine likeness with which man was created. (*NIV Study Bible 1984 Edition*, note on Mark 5:5, p. 1501)

3. What is missing in the townspeople's response to the healing of the miserable demon-possessed man?

4. What motivated their response?

> **Think About It:** Fear trumps opportunity in this incident in Jesus' ministry. Because of their fear of the unexplainable and their loss of income, the townspeople didn't care that the once miserable man was now completely normal. Nor did they bring their sick to be healed by the one who heals.

5. For what purpose did Jesus tell the man to go home?

6. *Heartbreak to Hope:* Read the quotes below. Reflect and respond on the statements that follow.

> "You can impress people at a distance; you can only impact them up close." (Howard Hendricks)
>
> "Relationships determine what we believe. We are talked into talking; we are loved into loving; we are related into believing." (Josh McDowell)

Relationships determine response. A loving relationship with a co-worker, neighbor, or family member just might stir that person to listen to your story and to accept the truth by which you live. That's why Jesus sent so many people home after their lives were changed. "Go to the ones with whom you have a relationship and introduce me to them." How has this truth impacted your life?

Respond to the Lord about what He's shown you today.

Day Two Study

Ask the Lord Jesus to speak to you through His Word. Tell Him that you are listening.

Read Mark 5:21-43.

What was the status of women in Jesus' day? In Greek/Roman society, women were generally given second-class status with few legal rights. In Jewish society, women had it better as they held a place of honor as wife and mother, especially if they had sons. At the birth of a son, all celebrated. At the birth of a daughter, there wasn't as much celebration. Jesus introduced a radically different value system. His compassion for women elevated their position in society and gave them equal relationship with Him. He spoke to women publicly, taught them openly, and defended them when they were criticized. He let them travel with Him and support Him with their own money. He never spoke condescendingly to women, made derogatory jokes about women, or humiliated them. No wonder they loved Him!

7. *Discover the Facts:* This is another "sandwich" section (vv. 21-24, vv. 25-34, and vv. 35-43).

    Who came to Jesus (v. 22), and what was his need?

> **Historical Insight:** A synagogue ruler is similar to an executive pastor in today's church settings. Jairus had a problem that neither his prominence nor his wealth could solve.

So Jesus went with Jairus, and the large crowd followed including a woman with a need. What do we know about her (vv. 25-26)?

Who or what brought her to Jesus (vv. 27-28)?

What happened when she reached out to Jesus (v. 29)?

What did Jesus say and do (vv. 30-32)?

How did the woman respond (v. 33)?

What did Jesus say to her (v. 34)?

Jairus was waiting during this interruption. He was informed that his daughter had died. Jesus continued to Jairus' house with only Peter, James, and John following Him. Once inside, what did Jesus do and say (vv. 40-41)?

What happened next (vv. 42-43)?

Scriptural Insight: Jesus awakened the little girl from the sleep of death. She was not resurrected with an immortal body. She would die again at some point in history. Jesus is the only one who has been resurrected from the dead.

8. Considering what the sick woman did not get to do or enjoy in her life because of her condition, in what ways could she now live in peace and be free from her suffering?

9. Jesus called her "daughter." How is this an application of Mark 3:35?

> **Think About It:** When Jesus insisted that she publicly reveal herself, He gave her hope for a new life. She could enter society and receive spiritual life. According to Ephesians 3:20, our God always does more than we ask or think!

10. After finding out that his daughter had died during the interruption, what did Jesus tell Jairus in v. 36? Read also Luke 8:50. What message was He giving to Jairus?

"Waiting" is prominent in this passage. The woman with the bleeding had to wait 12 years for relief and healing. Jairus had to wait an agonizingly long time through delays, diversions, and disappointing news. Jesus could have healed the girl from a distance, but He didn't. He stretched Jairus's faith through the waiting. God uses waiting to teach us to trust Him.

> **Scriptural Insight:** In the Old Testament, the Hebrew word translated "wait" (upon the Lord) means "to bind together" as in tying together loose ends. Waiting is rarely pleasant to us, but we make ourselves do it daily in various situations (doctor's offices, traffic, checkout lanes). Our focus is usually not on the waiting itself, but on the end result of the waiting. When it comes to waiting on the Lord, the Bible communicates a clear message: we are to do it, and it's good for us. Psalm 27:14 tells us waiting on the Lord will "strengthen your heart." Waiting on God brings us strength in all areas in our lives. It teaches us about Him and His timing. During those times of waiting, our ear is more attuned to the work of God. We also make ourselves available to talk with Him in prayer. When we seek God for a solution in our lives, these times of waiting strengthen our relationship with Him as we learn to rely on His timing and trust in His goodness. It binds us together with Him. (Lisa Jenkins-Moore, "Entwined in Him," *Living Magazine,* November 2016, pp. 16-17)

11. ***Heartbreak to Hope:*** We must usually wait for God's "always perfect" timing in answer to our prayers. Is this a problem for you? Have you become discouraged (or been discouraged in the past) from having to wait? Read the words to the song below. Consider that God is in the waiting, too, and that waiting binds you together with Him? How does this change your perspective of waiting?

Respond to the Lord about what He's shown you today.

Day Three Study

Ask the Lord Jesus to speak to you through His Word. Tell Him that you are listening.

Read Mark 6:1-6 (first part).

12. ***Discover the Facts:*** We are given more information about Jesus' hometown Nazareth and His family.

    Jesus began to teach in the synagogue in Nazareth. How did the listeners respond (v. 2)?

    What did they say about Jesus' earlier life and family (v. 3)?

    The crowd that was amazed also took offense at Him. Jesus declared that a prophet is not without honor except within his hometown. What did He not do and why (vv. 5-6)?

    Think About It: Jesus was a carpenter, a skilled craftsman, until He was 30 years old. In today's terms, he would be considered a blue-collar worker. He was a nobody in His hometown. If you do manual labor or are a craftsman, Jesus knows what your work is like. He understands it.

13. ***Heartbreak to Hope:*** Have you experienced rejection from your family or hometown similar to what Jesus experienced? He understands how you feel. Ask Him to show you how to respond to them next time you are disrespected or slandered by those who should appreciate you.

Who were Jesus' brothers?

Some church traditions hold that Mary had only one child, Jesus, and stayed a virgin for the rest of her life. Therefore, other siblings mentioned were either cousins or step-siblings (children of Joseph from a previous marriage) rather than half-siblings (children of Joseph and Mary together). Let's look at what the Bible actually says about this.

- Mark 6:3 (Mt 13:55)—this verse states plainly that Jesus had 4 brothers and at least 2 sisters. Interestingly, the townspeople who knew the family, calls them Jesus' brothers and sisters. The Greek word for *brother* refers to an actual biological brother, having a common mother and/or father. They had to have shared one biological parent for this word to apply. Since Joseph was not Jesus' biological father, the common biological parent had to be

Mary. Any attempt to make them cousins certainly violates a literal interpretation of the scripture, as does trying to make them step-siblings.

- Galatians 1:9—James is called the Lord's (Jesus's) *brother*, the same Greek word referenced above.

- John 7:5—the writer of this gospel, John (Jesus' cousin), calls them "His (Jesus's) own brothers" who did not believe in Him. John would know whether they were brothers or cousins. Again, the Greek for *brother* refers to a biological sibling. The interaction between Jesus and His brothers in this passage gives the impression that Jesus is the older, not the baby of the family.

- Acts 1:14—those present in the nucleus of the early church were Jesus' brothers.

- Matthew 1:25—Joseph kept Mary a virgin *until* Jesus' birth, a meaningless word unless it refers to Joseph and Mary beginning normal marital sexual relations after the birth. There is no scriptural evidence that Mary remained a virgin throughout her marriage.

- Luke 2:7—Jesus is called Mary's firstborn, implying that she had other children later.

But the most significant logical argument is that Joseph was legally eligible for David's throne. It was then through Joseph that Jesus was legally eligible for the throne. If Joseph had 4 sons older than Jesus, then the eldest of those sons (presumably James) would hold the legal title to the throne of David. This does not leave an option for Jesus to be the Messiah!

(Adapted from *The Bible Knowledge Commentary, New Testament,* pages 126-127, 208, 815; *NIV Study Bible 1984 Edition* notes; *Dr. Constable's Notes on Matthew and Mark*)

Read Mark 6:6-13.

14. ***Discover the Facts***: Jesus was on another tour of teaching from village to village. The disciples have been trained. Now, they are sent out to practice what they've learned.

    How were the Twelve sent out (v. 7)?

    How were they to travel (vv. 8-9)?

    Where were they to stay (vv. 10-11)?

    If they received opposition, what were they to do (v. 11)?

    Historical Insight: "Shaking the dust off their feet" was a symbolic act practiced by the Pharisees when they left an "unclean" Gentile area. Here it represented an act of warning to those who rejected God's message. (*NIV Study Bible 1984 Edition*, note on Matthew 10:14, p. 1456)

What did the Twelve do (vv. 12-13)?

Scriptural Insight: The people knew the difference between those who were sick and those who were demon-possessed. The gospel writers distinguished the differences for us as they wrote individual accounts. Yet, we are not told how they generally knew who was controlled by evil spirits rather than being infected with an illness.

15. As disciples of the rabbi Jesus, what did they do that mirrored what Jesus did?

Think About It: *Preparation* (being with Him, watching Him teach and work) added to *delegation* (doing it themselves with His authority to do so) produces *disciple-makers*.

16. Jesus instructed them not to take food, money or extra clothes. What would the disciples need to learn about God on their journey?

Scriptural Insight: Another time (Luke 22:35-36), Jesus tells them to take extra supplies. It is important that you do not take Jesus' instructions here as standard procedure for all ministry travels.

17. ***Heartbreak to Hope:*** In what areas of your life do you recognize God teaching you to trust Him for provision or protection?

Read Mark 6:14-29.

18. Who did the various groups of people think that Jesus was (vv. 14-16)?

19. What grabbed your attention from the account of John's death (vv. 17-29)?

> **Think About It:** Verse 20 is another example of blasphemy against the Holy Spirit. Herod was intrigued enough to listen to John and knew him to be a righteous and holy man. Yet, he remained unconvinced and unrepentant as was also his manipulative wife Herodias.

Respond to the Lord about what He's shown you today.

DAY FOUR STUDY

Ask the Lord Jesus to speak to you through His Word. Tell Him that you are listening.

Read Mark 6:30-46.

20. ***Discover the Facts***: The disciples return from their mission trip (vv. 7-13). They gathered around Jesus and reported to him all they had done and taught.

    What did Jesus want for them and why (v. 31)?

    Though they went by boat to a "solitary" place, a huge crowd followed and got there ahead of them. When He landed and saw the crowd, what was Jesus' response to them (v. 34)?

    What happened later in the day (vv. 35-36)?

    How did Jesus challenge His disciples (vv. 37-38)?

    What did Jesus do (vv. 39-41)?

What happened next (vv. 42-43)?

After the 5000 men plus their families were fed, what did Jesus do then (vv. 45-46)?

Think About It: Jesus gave His disciples the opportunity to learn how to serve people by challenging them to figure out how to find food for the people. And like a great coach, He talked them through it.

21. "They all ate and were satisfied" (v. 42).
    - What does it mean to be satisfied?

    - Read John 6:36. What does Jesus say about Himself?

    - Jesus looked upon the crowd as sheep needing a shepherd. Read Psalm 23:1-3. What does a good shepherd do for his sheep?

    Think About It: God did the multiplying of the bread and fish. Can God multiply your resources when you give thanks for what you have and offer it to Him?

22. Read John 6:14-15. What did the crowd want to do? In light of this, why do you think Jesus sent His disciples away?

LESSON 5

23. ***Heartbreak to Hope:*** Have you wanted to get away from the pressure for a while, either for yourself or with your family? Retreating to a quiet place and getting some rest is biblical. Take the time to get away with the Lord this week to get refreshed.

Read Mark 6:47-56.

24. ***Discover the Facts***: Let's look at the details in this familiar story.

　　By evening, the boat was in the middle of the Sea of Galilee. Jesus was alone on land (v. 47). What did Jesus notice and do (v. 48)?

　　How did the disciples react to seeing Jesus walking on water (vv. 49-50 first part)?

　　What did Jesus say to them (v. 50 second part)?

　　When Jesus climbed into the boat, the wind completely died down (v. 51). Why were they amazed (v. 52)?

　　When they landed at Gennesaret, what happened (vv. 53-56)?

　　Focus on the Meaning: The Twelve were still having trouble seeing Jesus as God. They were still thinking of Him as a rabbi or a prophet like Elijah or Elisha. Their lifelong concept of the Messiah was that of a warrior king like David had been. Jesus didn't fit that image.

25. Notice that Jesus' intention was to pass them by as they struggled (v. 48). What do you learn from this?

61

26. ***Heartbreak to Hope:*** Read Psalm 103:2-5. Our God promises to satisfy your heart's desires with good things, to fill you with everything you need to feel satisfied. As you reflect on Psalm 103:2-5, where in your life might you need Jesus to "satisfy your desires with good things?"

27. ***Heartbreak to Hope:*** Reflect back on this whole lesson, how did someone experiencing heartbreak, pain, or uncertainty find hope, healing and love?

Respond to the Lord about what He's shown you today.

Recommended: Listen to the podcast "Jesus Demonstrated God's Love for Women" after doing this lesson to reinforce what you have learned. Use the following listener guide.

LESSON 5

PODCAST LISTENER GUIDE

Jesus Demonstrated God's Love for Women

JESUS IS A PERSONAL GOD WHO BRINGS HOPE.

- When you look at what happened, you see that Jesus wouldn't allow "Dottie" to recede into the crowd without public assurance that she is permanently healed because of her faith. Jesus called her, "Daughter," indicating she had a new relationship with God plus so much more. God always does more than we ask or think. Jesus satisfied Dottie's heart with hope, healing, and love.

- As He took time out from His busy schedule to minister to two women personally, including a 12-year-old girl, Jesus demonstrated God's love for women so radically different from that of His culture.

JESUS DEMONSTRATED GOD'S LOVE FOR WOMEN.

- It was tough to be a woman living around the rim of the Mediterranean Sea at that time. In both Greek and Roman cultures, women held a second-rate status with few legal rights. Jewish women fared better than their Roman counterparts.

- The Lord Jesus demonstrated in His life on earth how much He loved and valued women. He taught them truth about God, forgave them for their sins, accepted them in His circle of followers, and gave new life to them after His resurrection. His care for them was so countercultural to what they had previously known.

- What you see in the Gospels is that Jesus never spoke condescendingly to women, never made derogatory jokes about them, nor did He ever humiliate them. Women who knew Him loved Him. They wanted to follow and serve Him! You can see all this in these 2 New Testament Women Bible studies: Live Out His Love and Satisfied by His Love.

- In the gospels, you see that Jesus treated women as no man had ever treated them before His time. His warmth, personal attention, tenderness, sound teaching, and compassion toward women were revolutionary.

JESUS IS THE ONE WHO UNDERSTANDS WOMEN

- As Creator, He designed us with a mind to know God, emotions to love God, and a will to obey God. That comes in the package we receive at birth.

- Our female minds need to be filled with the knowledge of Him so that our hearts may respond with great love for Him, and our wills can choose to obey Him.

- Jesus knows us backwards and forwards. He knows our emotional nature, our need for security and significance, and even our hormones! He understands our need to nurture and to be loved.

- A relationship with Jesus satisfies every spiritual need that you have. You don't need to go anywhere else to get those deep needs satisfied.

JESUS TEACHES US TO BE GOD-DEPENDENT WOMEN.

- Our God wants for us to be God-dependent women all the time. This is true for men too.

- Being God-dependent all the time is so radically different from what our western culture has taught us most of our lives—that we should not depend on anyone or anything for our success. To unlearn what we have learned might involve turning away from some voices in social media, channels, books, and blogs that contribute to the illusion that you are a stronger woman if you are totally self-reliant.

- How does this relying on God fit our lives as women today?
    - ✓ Being God-dependent doesn't mean we are supposed to stay like babies not doing anything for ourselves. We are supposed to grow and mature in our thinking and behavior.
    - ✓ Being God-dependent doesn't mean we are supposed to just lie back and let anything happen to us. The New Testament teaches Christians to be wise and proactive in our dealings with everyone—whether in the church or outside of it—for our own good as well as for the good of others.
    - ✓ Being God-dependent doesn't mean we are not supposed to use our skills, talents, advantages, and opportunities to be the best women we can be. Our God wants us to give back to Him all those skills, talents, advantages, and opportunities He has given to us and then use them for His glory.

- The key to being a God-dependent woman is dependent living. Whatever He brings into our lives that makes us more dependent upon Him is good for us.

    Human parents raise their children to be less dependent on them and more independent of them. But God raises His children to be less independent of Him and more dependent on Him.

- Dependent living is not weakness. It is being stronger and having more influence, success, and satisfaction than you could ever have through your own efforts.

- Because you know He loves you, you can have confidence in what the Lord Jesus Christ will do in your life so that you will want to depend on Him more than on yourself. You learn how to do this as you respond to God's love for you, act in obedience to the Word of God, depend on Jesus Christ for the power to do that, and trust Him with the results.

Let Jesus satisfy your heart with hope, healing, and love as you get to know Him and trust Him more each day.

Lesson 6: Clean, Unclean & Being "All In" or Nothing

(Mark 7:1-9:1)

Day One Study

Ask the Lord Jesus to speak to you through His Word. Tell Him that you are listening.

Read Mark 7:1-23

> **Focus on the Meaning:** I heard someone call the group of Pharisees and lawyers "The Bureau of Tapping and Snapping." They expected the people to do whatever they said without question, even if some of their traditions made no sense. The Pharisees had added many laws to the Law of Moses. These were called "traditions of the elders" and were often held in higher esteem than the Scriptures. The issue of washing hands when coming from the marketplace was not general cleaning of dirt but referred to an elaborate cleaning ritual that removed contamination from the Gentiles who were present in the public areas.

1. **Discover the Facts:** In today's passage, Jesus gets "in the face" of His hard-hearted opposition.

   What did the Pharisees and lawyers see (vv. 1-2)?

   What is their accusation (v. 5)?

   What did Jesus say in response to them (vv. 6-7)?

   What is His accusation (v. 8)?

   What example does Jesus give to prove His point (vv. 9-13)?

   What does He say they do to the commands of God (vv. 8, 9, 13)?

What does Jesus say to the crowd that nullifies the "traditions" and turns it into a heart issue (vv. 14-15)?

How does He explain this better to His disciples (vv. 18-19)?

What does make a person spiritually dirty (vv. 20-23)?

> **From the Greek:** The word *hypocrite* was a Greek theatrical term referring to an actor, a pretender. This was a commonly known cultural term. The actor would do one of two things: 1) hold a mask in front of his face while playing a part on the stage (one who hid his true self under a mask) or 2) contort and exaggerate facial expressions so the entire audience could see them, performing for recognition and applause. Jesus knew the Greek culture around Him and communicated with people in terms they understood.

2. The key issue Jesus expresses in vv. 20-23 is that of the heart. What is the "heart" of man?

> **Focus on the Meaning:** The list of sins in vv. 21-22 are not ranked by bad to worse. All sin is bad. Think of the most heinous crime. That's the ugliness of each one of these sins to God. The consequences are different, though. People and circumstances do not cause our sin. Those things reveal our hearts.

3. *Heartbreak to Hope:* Jesus told the Pharisees and lawyers that they let go, set aside, and nullify the commands of God for their own purposes. How do we do this today to fit in with our culture or our pleasures? Doing so will eventually lead to heartbreak of some kind as we reap the consequences of our actions.

Respond to the Lord about what He's shown you today.

DAY TWO STUDY

Ask the Lord Jesus to speak to you through His Word. Tell Him that you are listening.

Read Mark 7:24-30 and Matthew 15:21-26.

4. ***Discover the Facts***: Avoiding the hostility in Galilee, Jesus heads to Gentile territory. There He meets a woman who becomes a living example of the clean / unclean controversy.

   What was Jesus' plan (v. 24)?

   A woman heard about Him. What do we know about her and her situation (vv. 25-26)?

   What did she do and say?

   How did Jesus test her heart with His response (v. 27)?

   What in her response revealed her heart (v. 28)?

   What is Jesus' response (vv. 29-30, Matthew 15:28)?

   > **Scriptural Insight:** God desired to bless all people, but He purposed to bless humanity by first blessing the Jews (Genesis 12:3; Acts 3:26; Romans 1:16). In the gospels, Jesus restored Gentiles who came to Him in faith, not turning them away: the demon-possessed man (Mark 5:1-20, the Canaanite woman (Mark 7:24-30), and the Roman Centurion's servant (Matthew 8:5-13).

5. How did the woman demonstrate faith in what she did and said?

Think About It: Did you recognize her humility and tenaciousness? She basically told Jesus, "I recognize I have no rights. I don't deserve a thing, but I'm asking anyway." Jesus was pleased with what He saw in her faith.

6. Read 2 Chronicles 16:9. How does this incident in Jesus' ministry show that God doesn't play favorites? In what ways did He demonstrate grace to the woman?

7. **Heartbreak to Hope:** We all want to get away from such interruptions by needy people at times. Our responses may be governed by our time schedule, biases, and even hard hearts. We cannot meet every need. But who can meet the spiritual needs of every person? Put yourself in the disciples' shoes, what should they have done for that woman instead of trying to send her away? What can you do when faced with a need?

Read Mark 7:31-37.

> **Historical Insight:** The Decapolis was a league of 10 independent cities characterized by Greek culture. All but one of them were located east of the Sea of Galilee and the Jordan River. This was Gentile territory. The healed man from Mark 5:19-20 lived there.

8. What grabbed your attention as you read this passage?

9. What truth was Jesus communicating to these Gentile people when He looked up to heaven as He healed the man (v. 34)?

10. **Heartbreak to Hope:** What in today's lesson speaks to your heart?

Respond to the Lord about what He's shown you today.

Day Three Study

Ask the Lord Jesus to speak to you through His Word. Tell Him that you are listening.

Read Mark 8:1-10.

11. Fill out the chart below comparing the feeding of the 5000 (Mark 6) with the feeding of the 4000 (Mark 8).

What is similar?	What is different?
vv. 2-3	
vv. 4-5	
vv. 6-7	
v. 8	
v. 9	

Jesus felt compassion for the crowds. He chose to be kind to them by taking care of not only their spiritual needs through His amazing teaching but also their physical needs through food. Kindness is being tender-hearted plus doing something to meet a need.

12. ***Heartbreak to Hope:*** In what ways do you try to be kind? Are you kind in your charity? Do you give what will actually benefit others or just to clean out your closet and pantry? Our kindness lets other people see God as kind and tender-hearted, compassionate. Jot down 2 ways that you can be kind to someone in your sphere of influence specifically this week.

Read Mark 8:11-21.

13. ***Discover the Facts:*** Jesus is back on the west side of the Sea of Galilee. The Pharisees tested Jesus by asking for a sign from heaven. Jesus sighed deeply and gave them no sign.

On the way back across the lake, the disciples realized they had forgotten to bring bread except for one loaf. What warning did Jesus give to them (v. 15)?

What did they hear (v. 16)?

Aware of their discussion, of what does Jesus remind them (vv. 17-21)?

Focus on the Meaning: Confirmation is repeatedly put forth that Jesus was and is the Messiah, and He was given complete authority by God here on earth to heal, conquer death, and to forgive us of our sins. This evidence disclaims the statement, "If only I could see a miracle, then I would believe in God." The Pharisees and other Jews experienced and/or witnessed many miracles first-hand performed by Jesus. Yet, many still did not believe Him to be the Messiah or understand His message. Faith is not based on seeing. It is based on believing.

14. Jesus' words in v. 15 are like a parent mulling over an incident and dispensing advice to children. What was He trying to tell them?

Think About It: Did you think to yourself when you read the Pharisees' question (v. 11), "Weren't healings and feedings enough?" I certainly did. What did they really want? Perhaps they wanted Jesus to call fire down from heaven like Elijah did in 1 Kings 18. But then, would that have convinced them? I doubt it. Their hearts were too hard. We, too, must beware of seeking "signs" different from what God has already shown us.

15. *Heartbreak to Hope:* Look at the disciples' focus in vv. 14, 16. Do you do this? In what ways do you fret about something small and forget all about the power and teachings of the One who is always with you? Ask Jesus to help you stay focused on Him and His goodness to you.

Read Mark 8:22-26.

16. What grabbed your attention as you read this passage?

17. Have you noticed that Jesus took different actions to heal people? Jesus didn't heal according to a formula. Sometimes He just spoke for it to be done; other times He touched, spit, and spoke. What would be a good reason for Him mixing things up like that?

Respond to the Lord about what He's shown you today.

Day Four Study

Ask the Lord Jesus to speak to you through His Word. Tell Him that you are listening.

Read Mark 8:27-30.

18. ***Discover the Facts***: Now Jesus and His disciples are way up north of Galilee near the foot of Mt. Hermon. It's retreat time again.

    When Jesus asked His disciples who people say that He is, what is their response (v. 28)?

    How does Peter answer the personal question, "Who do you say I am?"

    What does Jesus tell them?

    Scriptural Insight: In Matthew 16:13-19, we learn that Peter's answer was revealed by God. Jesus calls Simon *petros*, meaning "stone, a piece of a bigger rock." The bigger rock is the apostles and prophets who know that Jesus is the Christ, the Son of the living God. Christ will build His Church on that foundation. And nothing, including the gates of Hell, will be able to stop the onslaught of the people of God to build the Church. Peter is given the keys of the kingdom, which we later understand meant that he would be present to open doors to the 3 different people groups—the Jews in Acts 2, the Samaritans (half-Jews) in Acts 8, and the Gentiles in Acts 10. The apostles are given the power of binding and loosing. That is not referring to forgiving sins or determining eternal destiny (as in cults or used by the medieval church). It is the ability to authoritatively state what is permitted or forbidden in terms of practices as in Acts 15 and 1 Corinthians 7.

Read Mark 8:31-9:1.

19. ***Discover the Facts:*** We are now at a turning point in Mark. Jesus begins to reveal the future to His disciples to prepare them for what's ahead.

    What does He teach them (v. 31)?

    When Peter takes Him aside and rebukes Him for what He is saying, how does Jesus respond (v. 33)?

    To the crowd and the disciples, what does Jesus say (vv. 34-35)?

    How does He explain this in vv. 36-37?

    What promise does Jesus make in 9:1?

    Focus on the Meaning: 1) *Denying oneself* does not mean denying your personality, living as an ascetic, or neglecting your physical needs. It does mean saying "no" to selfish interests and earthly securities and turning away from the idolatry of self-centeredness. Following Jesus involves denying your own way of approaching life and adopting God's way of approaching life. It is a daily choice of obeying God. 2) *Taking up one's cross* does not mean to purposely suffer or stoically bear life's troubles as though having no choices. Carrying the cross in Roman-occupied territory demonstrated submission to the authority against which one had previously rebelled. When Jesus took up His cross, He was submitting to the authority of God and obeying Him. So taking up your cross represents obedience to God and whatever opportunity or adversity that brings to you. Your choice is this: "I am God's, or I am my own." You can't have it both ways.

20. Because of the phrase "adulterous and sinful generation," we know that Jesus is addressing those in the crowd who are listening to Him but resisting belief in Him.

    - What does it mean to be ashamed?

    - What would it look like for someone to be ashamed of Christ and His Words?

21. ***Heartbreak to Hope:*** Revelation demands a response. Jesus is the Son of God, calling you to follow Him—to approach life God's way rather than your own way or the world's way. Choosing His way is rewarding.

    - What rewards have you received from choosing God's way of doing life over the world's way?

    - What challenges have you faced for choosing God's way of doing life over the world's way?

22. ***Heartbreak to Hope:*** Reflect back on this whole lesson, how did someone experiencing heartbreak, pain, or uncertainty find hope, healing and love?

Respond to the Lord about what He's shown you today.

Recommended: Listen to the podcast "Dare to Be Different from Your World" after doing this lesson to reinforce what you have learned. Use the following listener guide.

PODCAST LISTENER GUIDE

Dare to Be Different from Your World

"Whoever wants to be my disciple must deny themselves and take up their cross and follow me. For whoever wants to save their life will lose it, but whoever loses their life for me and for the gospel will save it." (Mark 8:34-35)

DARE TO BE DIFFERENT FROM THE WORLD.

- "To dare" means to "have the courage to do something." Jesus was daring His followers to be different from the world around us knowing it's for our own good. And we are to do this by faith, like everything else in our Christian life.

  "Therefore, I urge you, brothers and sisters, in view of God's mercy, to offer your bodies as a living sacrifice, holy and pleasing to God—this is your true and proper worship. Do not conform to the pattern of this world, but be transformed by the renewing of your mind. Then you will be able to test and approve what God's will is—his good, pleasing and perfect will." (Romans 12:1-2)

1) DARE TO EVALUATE.

- We can learn 3 things from Romans 12:2:
  - ✓ For every child of God, conforming to the world's pattern is not a good thing because we are told to stop it.
  - ✓ We have a choice to not conform to this world.
  - ✓ Somehow, we need to figure out if we are conforming to this world or not. That requires evaluation.

- If you want to dare to be different, you've first got to dare to evaluate your life. Where are you being pulled by the world's influence and ideas? What advantages or disadvantages have shaped your thinking and your character? What is God showing you about yourself as you read His Word?

2) DARE TO SUBMIT.

We are to dare to submit to being transformed, to trust ourselves to Jesus' transforming power.

First step: Recognize that all of you belongs to God anyway, and "daring to submit" to Him pleases God and is for your good. Romans 12:1

- Offering our bodies means to present the totality of our life and activities to Him.

- You decide to be Jesus' disciple. A disciple is an active follower or learner. Jesus Christ calls us to follow Him as His disciples, committed to learning from Him and becoming like Him as we intentionally apply to our lives what He teaches us through His Word and what He allows into our lives.

Second step: Renew your mind from the world's way of thinking, feeling, & doing to God's way of thinking, feeling, & doing. Romans 12:2

- Renewing means to push the conforming influences away from you and to replace them with spiritual input from God's Word, from prayer, and from friendship with Christians who love God.

- Have you recognized the conforming influences on you? Are you putting them away from you and replacing them with God's Word, prayer, and friendships with godly Christians? Where is your mental energy going?

    "People pay attention to what they deem important. And many Christians invest more of their mental energy in cultural literacy than in biblical literacy." (George Barna, *Dallas Morning News*, Saturday, Dec. 2, 2006.)

- Jesus warned His followers about being choked by the cares and riches of this world in the Parable of the Sower. He called for His disciples to be willing to sacrifice their own pursuits in order to put Him first. New Testament writers encouraged Jesus' disciples to work hard not only to provide their own needs but also to be able to generously share with others. That requires sacrifice. *Matthew 6:33; Mark 4:18-19; Luke 9:57-62; 2 Corinthians 8-9; Ephesians 4:28*

3) DARE TO EXPECT RESULTS.

#1. Priorities get changed.

- When you desire to be Jesus' disciple, committed to Him, priorities in your life get changed. Ask the Lord Jesus what needs to get changed in your life, in your daily activity, in your plans. He will show you. You can trust Him. Your priorities will get changed.

#2. Character gets changed.

There are two aspects of being transformed to the likeness of Christ.

- *God's part:* Working according to His will and purpose for your life. God will complete His work so that you will be like Jesus in your future. God puts into your heart the desire to be like Jesus so you will want it too. And God gives you everything you need to be godly.

- *Your part:* Renewing your mind through studying God's words in the Bible to see how to approach life His way. Your part also involves having a desire for God's work in you to give you the character of Christ. When you long for His work in your life, you will want to submit to what He is doing and ask for Him to change you. Jesus modeled for us how to approach life God's way and how to live in dependence upon Him in the process.

By faith, you can dare to be different from the world. Trust Him to help you do that in your life.

Let Jesus satisfy your heart with hope, healing, and love as you get to know Him and trust Him more each day.

Lesson 7: Glory, Honesty, & Serious Pride Issues

(Mark 9:2-10:52)

In Mark 9 and 10, Jesus addresses a bunch of heart attitude adjustments His followers need to make based on what He told them in Mark 8:34. Deny yourself and listen to Him (God confirms this one!).

Day One Study

Ask the Lord Jesus to speak to you through His Word. Tell Him that you are listening.

Read Mark 9:1-13.

1. ***Discover the Facts***: What Jesus promised in 9:1 comes true for three of the Twelve.

    Jesus took Peter, James, and John with Him to the mountain. What happened there (vv. 2-3)? See also Matthew 17:2.

    Who showed up, and what were they doing (v. 4)? See also Luke 9:31.

    What is Peter's response to what he saw (vv. 5-6)?

    What is God's response to Peter and the others (v. 7)?

    As they were coming down the mountain, Jesus told them not to tell anyone about that experience yet. They were discussing what "rising from the dead" meant. Then, asked Jesus about Elijah's coming. What is Jesus' response (vv. 12-13)?

    Scriptural Insight: An angel told John the Baptist's parents that their son *"would go before the Lord and minister in the spirit and power of Elijah, to...make ready a people prepared for the Lord" (Luke 1:17).* Jesus explains in Matthew 11:14 that John the Baptist would have been the Elijah who was to come had the Israelites believed Christ was the Messiah. The religious leaders, however, would not accept God's way that was being proclaimed by Jesus and John. So in essence, the prophecy was only partially fulfilled. John the Baptist did fulfill the part about being the Messiah's forerunner (Malachi 3:1; 4:5). But the people's hearts were hard, and they did not turn their hearts toward God.

2. What is being revealed through the transfiguration? See also Philippians 2:6-7 and 2 Corinthians 4:6.

3. **Heartbreak to Hope:** What confirmation does the presence of Moses and Elijah give to us as believers? Are you confident that there is life with God beyond the grave for you? If you have placed your faith in Jesus Christ, you are guaranteed eternal life with God after you die. Read John 5:24 for that confirmation.

Read Mark 9:14-32.

> **Scriptural Insight:** At this point in Mark's gospel, Jesus had foretold His arrest, death, and resurrection to His disciples four times. The women who followed Him also heard Him speak of this upcoming event (Luke 24:8).

4. **Discover the Facts:** Off the mountain and back to real life, Jesus responds to a father's need and the disciples' lack.

    What is the situation (vv. 17-18)?

    The boy has been like this since childhood. The father asks Jesus to take pity on them and heal his son "if" Jesus can. How does Jesus respond to that (v. 23)?

    How does the father respond to Jesus (v. 24)?

> **Scriptural Insight:** We have seen Jesus drive out demons from many people in His ministry. But not all troubles He encountered were caused by demons. Having an unhealthy focus on demons can be dangerous and distracting for believers. Instead, choose to be Jesus-conscious rather than demon-conscious. Jesus is greater than all angels, including Satan and his demons. Jesus lives in you through His Holy Spirit — God is in you. Demons have no authority over you. You should be aware that they exist and beware of their deceptive nature. Bad things can happen because we live in a broken world or because people make bad choices. Demons are not behind everything bad that happens. For example, the Bible does not say that the storms in Mark 4 and 6 were demonic.

The disciples had driven out evil spirits when Jesus sent them on mission (Mark 6:12-13). Jesus' answer in Mark 9:29 implies that they didn't pray before trying to drive out the demon. Perhaps their success in the past led them to think they could handle this themselves. But they could not. That is the danger of success.

> **Think About It:** Here is a key truth. Human parents raise their children to become more independent and less dependent on them. God raises His children to become more dependent on Him and less independent of Him.

5. *Heartbreak to Hope:* Experiencing success makes us most vulnerable to becoming self-sufficient, unguarded against temptation, uncorrectable or unteachable, and complacent. Have you experienced this in your life? You can overcome that by recognizing your vulnerability, confessing your need for God, and renewing your dependence on God.

Respond to the Lord about what He's shown you today.

Day Two Study

Ask the Lord Jesus to speak to you through His Word. Tell Him that you are listening.

Read Mark 9:33-37.

6. *Discover the Facts:* Another teachable moment lies ahead for the disciples.

   What did Jesus notice (v. 33)?

   What is the disciples' response (v. 34)?

   Taking advantage of this teachable moment, what does Jesus do and say (vv. 35-37)?

7. What is Jesus trying to communicate to the Twelve about their role as servant leaders?

Think About It: To achieve His purposes, God chooses to use nobodies (like the disciples) to display His power and grace as they rely on Him. He chooses to use somebodies (like Paul) when they give up dependence on their natural abilities and resources to rely on Him. Either way, the key is dependence on Him.

Read Mark 9:38-41.

8. Summarize what you just read.

Think About It: Someone described this example as being on the same team but in different positions. Could this apply to denominational divisions in our modern world? As long as all believe that Jesus is the Christ, the Son of God, they are on the same team. What do you think?

Read Mark 9:42-50.

9. Jesus uses a lot of exaggeration in this passage to make a point for His disciples. Relate what He teaches here to the dissension and competition expressed in vv. 33-41.

10. What truth is expressed in v. 48?

11. *Heartbreak to Hope:* What in today's lesson speaks to your heart?

Respond to the Lord about what He's shown you today.

Day Three Study

> **Scriptural Insight:** Between 9:50 and 10:1, Mark left out a lot of Jesus' ministry activities. You can read Luke 10-18 and John 7-10 to fill in the gap.

Read Mark 10:1-12.

Ask the Lord Jesus to speak to you through His Word. Tell Him that you are listening.

12. ***Discover the Facts:*** Jesus is leaving Galilee for the last time, heading to the south.

    What is the test question from the Pharisees this time (v. 2)?

    How does Jesus respond (v. 3)?

    After hearing their answer, what does Jesus teach them about God's intention (vv. 5-9)?

    What additional explanation does Jesus give to His disciples (vv. 11-12)?

    > **Scriptural Insight:** The certificates of divorce referenced in Deuteronomy 24 were given to protect the rights of women. Women abandoned by their husbands would be left destitute in that culture. The certificate of divorce allowed them to remarry. Jesus stressed that God created man and woman at the beginning of creation (Genesis 1) and instituted marriage between a man and a woman at that time as a covenant (Genesis 2). Divorce was permitted after the act of adultery by one spouse because that violates the covenant and breaks the marriage bond (Matthew 19:9). Is divorce lawful? Yes. Is it God's will? No. Is adultery covered by the cross? Yes. Is remarriage honored by God? Yes, it is a covenant recognized by God.

Read "Principles of Marriage and Divorce" in the RESOURCES section for additional insight.

Read Mark 10:13-16.

13. ***Discover the Facts:*** Jesus loves the little children. People were bringing little children to Jesus for him to place his hands on them.

    How did the disciples react (v. 13)?

    What does Jesus feel and then say to His disciples (v. 14)?

What does He then do to demonstrate what He just said?

Think About It: Jesus not only blessed the children (what the parents wanted), but He also took them in His arms and put His hands on them while blessing them. Our God always does more than we ask.

14. How does anyone receive the kingdom of God like a little child?

Focus on the Meaning: Do little children go to heaven when they die? Mark 10:14 is a verse that gives us confidence that they do. We can conclude this not because they have been baptized or because the parents are believers. It is not because children are innocent of sin or that they are not morally accountable. The kingdom of heaven belongs to little children. It is their property. Since Scripture only addresses the issue of adults as believers or unbelievers, it can be surmised that the salvation of babies and small children is God's concern, not ours. We can be confident that children go to heaven when they die because the blood of Jesus Christ was provided for their account. Young children have not rejected the blood of Jesus. It is there to cover their sins, washing them clean, And it is the character of God to apply that blood even though they cannot believe for themselves because they are too young. For more information, go to backtothebible.org/is-my-child-in-heaven.

15. ***Heartbreak to Hope:*** Jesus said, "Let the little children come to me, and do not hinder them, for the kingdom of God belongs to such as these."

- How do we help children come to Him?

- How do we hinder children from coming to Him?

Read Mark 10:17-31.

16. ***Discover the Facts:*** Jesus issues a tough challenge to a young man.

What is the young man's question in v. 17?

What is Jesus' response (vv. 18-19)?

How does the man confidently answer (v. 20)?

Jesus feels love for this man. What challenge does He give that reveals his true need (v. 21)?

Scriptural Insight: Jesus asked the rich young ruler to surrender his fortune in order to know true riches (Mark 10:21). He asked the young boy to surrender his meager lunch so that thousands could feast (John 6:5-13). He asked the disciples to surrender their plans, their dreams, their very lives, to follow Him (Matthew 4:18-22, Luke 5:1-22). And He asks us to surrender our rights, our reputation, our possessions, and our security. He wants our dreams and desires, our losses and our loves. Why? Because He knows that what He offers is better by far than anything we are holding onto. He knows that surrendering everything we have and everything we are to Him yields joy, purpose and peace that we cannot possess any other way. He knows that when we put our pain, loss and regret into His loving hands we will finally begin to experience the healing and the hope we long for. (Woven, *The Truth about Redemption Next Step*, "Redeeming Hope: Your journey Toward Surrender")

17. Summarize Jesus' explanation to His disciples (vv. 23-27)? See also Mark 9:23.

Focus on the Meaning: In their mind, money equals blessings from God. If the rich man who has supposedly been blessed by God can't be saved by doing good works, how can any of the rest of us poor folks ever be saved? We know the answer is by faith alone, not works.

18. What is the reward for transferring your allegiance from people and material comforts to Jesus and the gospel He preaches (vv. 29-31)?

19. *Heartbreak to Hope:* What in today's lesson speaks to your heart?

Respond to the Lord about what He's shown you today.

Day Four Study

Ask the Lord Jesus to speak to you through His Word. Tell Him that you are listening.

Read Mark 10:32-45.

20. ***Discover the Facts:*** After spending quite a bit of time avoiding Jerusalem, Jesus is now leading the way to that city, astonishing the Twelve with another prediction of what would happen to Him there. Then comes another teachable moment for them. If you remember the "Who is the greatest?" conversation (Mark 9:34), it picks up again here.

    Who comes to Jesus and with what request (vv. 35-37)? See also Matthew 20:20.

    What is Jesus' reply (v. 38)?

    After James and John boldly declare they can "drink the cup" (of suffering), Jesus affirms that they will do so. But what can He not promise (v. 40)?

    When the other ten heard about this, they became indignant with James and John. Jesus calls them together for a teachable moment. How does the world structure authority (v. 42)?

    But how should it be for the servants of Jesus (vv. 43-44)?

    Write v. 45 in the space below. This is considered the key verse for Mark.

    Scriptural Insight: Matthew wrote that their mother, Salome, the sister of Jesus' mother, voiced their request for them (Matthew 20:20). Mark put the words in their own mouths, because the request came from their hearts, even though Salome may have spoken them. Perhaps they thought their family connection with Jesus justified their request. James and John were Jesus' cousins (cf. Matthew 27:55-56; Mark 15:40; John 19:25). Frequently rulers appointed close family members to important government positions. (*Dr. Constable's Notes on Mark 2017 Edition*, p. 158)

21. How did Jesus serve while He was on earth?

22. What does He mean when He says that He gives His life as a ransom for many?

> **Focus on the Meaning:** What Jesus did for us is called "redemption." Redemption means to set something or someone free from bondage by paying a ransom. Jesus' blood was the purchase price that redeemed us from our bondage to sin. We can now choose to obey our new master who has greater power living inside of us—the Spirit of God Himself—who can give us freedom from any entrapping sin. We have also been released into freedom to serve God in obedience, as He leads us to do what is good out of hearts of love and gratitude.

23. *Heartbreak to Hope:* Servant leadership is powerful in God's business. Jesus described a servant leader as one who served those within her influence to lead them more than lording over them with her power. How can you be a servant leader in your sphere of influence—at work, at home, at church, and in the community? What would that look like?

Read Mark 10:46-52.

24. What grabbed your attention in this passage?

25. Look at Mark 10:36 and 10:51 where Jesus asked the same question of different people. Contrast the motives of the individuals involved.

26. **Heartbreak to Hope:** Reflect back on this whole lesson, how did someone experiencing heartbreak, pain, or uncertainty find hope, healing and love?

Respond to the Lord about what He's shown you today.

Recommended: Listen to the podcast "Treasuring the Gift of Jesus Christ" after doing this lesson to reinforce what you have learned. Use the following listener guide.

LESSON 7

PODCAST LISTENER GUIDE

Treasuring the Gift of Jesus Christ

CHRISTIANITY IS CHRIST

- Christianity is Christ! It is not a lifestyle. It's not rules of conduct. It's not a society of people who have joined together by the sprinkling or covering of water. Christianity is a relationship with the Lord Jesus Christ.

WHAT JESUS CLAIMED ABOUT HIMSELF

- Not only did Jesus claim to be God, but He also claimed to be the answer to the needs of the human heart. He consistently calls God His father. He declared His right to judge and said that He deserves the honor that belongs to God.

- Jesus consistently calls God His father. He declared His right to judge and said that He deserves the honor that belongs to God. Those are pretty radical statements. The works He was doing could only be done by God.

- Even in His trials before the Jewish and Roman leaders, Jesus clearly and boldly claimed His identity as the promised anointed one of God. He claimed to be the Son of Man who was also the Son of God.

JESUS WAS FULLY HUMAN.

- Jesus was fully human. He experienced the normal process of body development from a child to an adult man. He obeyed His parents and learned to live with at least 4 brothers and 2 sisters. In His human body, Jesus felt hunger and thirst, tears and anger, distress and pain.

- Because Jesus was fully human, He understands every single one of your heartaches, physical pains, feelings of rejection, strained relationships, abuse, grief, and impatience. He gets your joy too.

- Jesus was fully human, but He did not sin because He lived in perfect love for God the Father, His Father. Because He loved God perfectly, He lived in perfect dependence on God the Father and perfect obedience. And He gave us a pattern to follow so that we can learn to love God and to depend upon Him by faith too.

JESUS WAS FULLY GOD.

- Jesus is the image of the invisible God. He is the exact representation of God's likeness. We're not talking about His face but His character. *Colossians 1:15; John 14:9*

- Jesus as the Son of God is the firstborn **over** all creation. This refers to Him being the one who had priority and supremacy over everything that God the Father owned. He inherited all of it. *Colossians 1:15*

- Jesus was the Creator. He was not created. All things were created by Him and through Him. *Colossians 1:16; John 1:3*

- Jesus holds all things together. Christ is the controlling and unifying force in nature. *Colossians 1:17; Hebrews 1:3*

- Jesus is also Head of the Church. The Jews and Gentiles are combined into one body of believers, and He is the Head of that body. *Colossians 1:18*

- All God's fullness dwells in Jesus. The totality of God's powers and attributes are in Jesus. There is nothing missing. There is nothing more of God that we can get apart from Jesus. *Colossians 1:19*

JESUS IS LORD OVER ALL.

- Jesus Christ is fully God and is Lord over all. Jesus not only claimed Psalm 110:1 for Himself but also demonstrated that He was the Son of God who sits at God's right hand. Jesus is the Christ. He is also the Lord. Lord means master.

- As fully God and fully man, you can be confident that Jesus as human understands how you feel and is powerful enough as God to take care of your every need. When you go to Him in prayer, you can trust that He understands, that He knows how you are feeling and what your needs are at that moment. You can trust His compassion toward you to meet your needs. Are you confident of that?

- Jesus invites you to trust in what He says about Himself—that He is the Son of God—and believe that He died on the cross for you. Have you done that?

- As soon as you trust in Christ to be your Savior, you begin a loving relationship with the God of the universe. From then on, you have a new spiritual life with God's Spirit living inside you and producing many new qualities in you as you respond to Him.

- You receive complete love and acceptance by God as your Father. You receive treasure that is yours to know and experience for the rest of your earthly life. When you trust in Christ, He is in your life forever. You will never be without him. Ever.

- The treasure that God offers you in Jesus Christ is greater than anything you could substitute for Him. Why not spend the rest of your life getting to know this Jesus who gave Himself for you so you could have a new life? As God the Father said, "Listen to Him!"

Let Jesus satisfy your heart with hope, healing, and love as you get to know Him and trust Him more each day.

Lesson 8: A Parade, Housecleaning, and Lots of Tests!

(Mark 11:1-12:44)

DAY ONE STUDY

Ask the Lord Jesus to speak to you through His Word. Tell Him that you are listening.

Read Mark 11:1-11.

1. ***Discover the Facts:*** By comparing the four gospels, we can determine that Jesus got to Bethany on Friday and rested on Saturday (the Sabbath). Now it's time for Him to present Himself to His people. Expectations are high!

   Jesus sent two of His disciples into town for a donkey colt. They find it exactly as Jesus promised. When they brought the colt to Jesus, what did the disciples do (v. 7)?

   What did the people do for Jesus (v. 8)?

   What did they shout (vv. 9-10)? See also Psalm 118:25-26.

   Jesus accepted their worship. Then, what did He do (v. 11)? See also Luke 19:41-44.

   From the Greek: *Hosanna* (Greek) comes from *hosiahna* (Hebrew) meaning "O save us now," a prayer addressed to God. Over time, it became a shout of praise like "Hallelujah." Chanting "Hosanna" and "Hosanna in the highest" became part of the traditional Passover celebration. The Jews seeing Jesus on the donkey entering Jerusalem were filled with hope that Jesus was their promised Messiah.

2. What was Jesus deliberately doing now that He had been avoiding before this?

HEARTBREAK TO HOPE: GOOD NEWS FROM MARK

Read Mark 11:12-26.

3. ***Discover the Facts***: This is another "sandwich" section—vv. 12-14 and vv. 20-26 are related. The clearing of the Temple comes in the middle.

   After confronting the fig tree, Jesus headed to the Temple. In the Court of the Gentiles at the Temple, what four things did Jesus do (vv. 15-16)?

   Of what did He remind those watching and listening (v. 17)?

   How did the religious leaders take Jesus' actions (v. 18)?

   After spending the night outside of Jerusalem, what did they see the next morning (v. 20)?

   > **Scriptural Insight:** A marketplace atmosphere existed in the court of the Gentiles, the outermost courtyard within the temple enclosure (Gr. *hieron*, cf. v. 17). During Passover season, pilgrims could buy sacrificial animals and change their money on the Mount of Olives, so there was no need to set up facilities to do these things in the temple courtyard—which Caiaphas [the High Priest] had done. Jesus' literal housecleaning represented His authority as Messiah to clean up the corrupt nation of Israel. Verse 16, unique in Mark, shows the extent to which Jesus went in purifying the temple. [They were using the Temple courts as a shortcut to the Roman highway outside of town.] (*Dr. Constable's Notes on Mark 2017 Edition,* p. 168)

4. The fig tree became an object lesson. It represented Israel. Jesus' request of fruit from it represented His presence and the last chance before Israel would be judged as fruitless. Jesus then used hyperbole (exaggeration) to illustrate some things about faith and prayer in vv. 22-25 that are impossible without God. What does He tell them?

   > **Focus on the Meaning:** We must beware of taking v. 24 out of context. Rather than explaining the symbolic significance of the cursing of the fig tree, Jesus proceeded to focus on the means by which the miracle happened. ... The point was that dependent trust in God can accomplish humanly impossible things through prayer (cf. James 1:6). God is the source of the power to change. "Moving a mountain" is a universal symbol of doing

something that appears to be impossible (cf. Zechariah 4:7). Jesus presupposed that overcoming the difficulty in view was God's will. A true disciple of Jesus would hardly pray for anything else (Matthew 6:10). The person praying can therefore believe that what he requests will happen because it is God's will. He will neither doubt God's ability to do what he requests, since God *can* do anything, nor will he doubt that God *will* grant his petition, since it is God's will. He will not have a divided heart about this matter. (*Dr. Constable's Notes on Mark 2017 Edition*, p. 170)

What the merchants were doing at the Temple is similar to having Facebook ads on the screens in a church service today during communion and prayer time. It would distract people from worshiping God. Can churches offer books and tickets for sale in the lobby? Yes. God's temple now is the gathered people not the building (see 1 Corinthians 3:16, directed to the community not individuals). The building is not God's house; it's just a building used by the people of God for gathering together. And yes, we should be cognizant of first impressions when people visit our building.

5. **Heartbreak to Hope:** What in today's lesson speaks to your heart?

Respond to the Lord about what He's shown you today.

Day Two Study

Ask the Lord Jesus to speak to you through His Word. Tell Him that you are listening.

Read Mark 11:27-33.

6. **Discover the Facts**: Now begins a series of tests for Jesus, trying to make Him do something that changes the popular opinion of Him. Here's Test #1.

    While Jesus was walking in the temple courts, the chief priests, the teachers of the law and the elders came to him. What is their question (v. 28)?

    Jesus answers with a question of His own. What is it (vv. 29-30)?

    How do the leaders respond (vv. 31-32)?

Then, what does Jesus say?

> **Think About It:** The religious leaders issued the challenge but weren't really interested in the answer. This is a case of intellectual dishonesty. Do you know anyone like that?

Read Mark 12:1-12.

7. Instead of answering their question, Jesus tells a parable that reveals their motives and lets them know the consequences of their actions before they even take them. This parable has recognizable parts to it. The listeners knew exactly what Jesus was saying.

   A man planted a vineyard, then rented it to some tenants. What did the tenants do to everyone sent by the owner?

   What did they do to the son of the owner?

   What then will the owner of the vineyard do?

   What does Jesus declare in vv. 10-11?

   How does what Jesus say in the parable connect with Mark 11:28?

   How did the religious leaders respond (v. 12)?

   > **Think About It:** Hard hearts don't change with kindness, challenges, warnings, or consequences. Hard hearts can only be changed from the inside by one's decision to give up rebellion against God and submit to His authority. Jesus shot an arrow directly at their need to submit their authority to God and recognize Jesus as being sent from Him.

Respond to the Lord about what He's shown you today.

Day Three Study

Ask the Lord Jesus to speak to you through His Word. Tell Him that you are listening.

Read Mark 12:13-17.

8. ***Discover the Facts***: Here comes Test #2. Actually, these are more like traps than tests.

    The Pharisees sent some of the Pharisees and Herodians to Jesus to test Him. What do they admit about Him (v. 14)?

    What is their test question?

    Jesus knows about their hypocrisy and attempt to trap Him. What is Jesus' response (vv. 15-16)?

    Then, how does He answer their test question (v. 17)?

    What is their response?

    > **Historical Insight:** Since Judea had become a Roman province in A.D. 6, the Romans had required the Jews to pay a yearly "poll (head) tax" into the emperor's treasury. The Zealots later refused to pay it, claiming that payment acknowledged Rome's right to rule over them. The Pharisees paid it but objected strongly to it. The Herodians paid it willingly since they supported Roman rule. (*Dr. Constable's Notes on Mark 2017 Edition*, pp. 176-177)

9. The "Caesar" part we can figure out. But what do you think Jesus meant when He said, give "to God what is God's?"

Read Mark 12:18-27.

> **Historical Insight:** The "Sadducees" were mainly urban, wealthy, and educated Jews. Their numbers were comparatively few, but they occupied important positions including many in the priesthood. Their influence was greater than their size as a party within Judaism. This is the only place Mark mentioned them. They claimed to believe only what the Old Testament taught, and they did not follow the traditions of the elders that the Pharisees observed. They did not believe in the "resurrection," because they said they could find no clear revelation about it in the Old Testament. (*Dr. Constable's Notes on Mark 2017 Edition*, p. 178)

10. **Discover the Facts:** We are now at Test (Trap) #3.

    The Sadducees present a hypothetical situation about a woman with multiple husbands. What is their test question (v. 23)?

    Jesus declares that they are in error because they do not know the Scriptures or the power of God. Then, He presents them with what truth in v. 25?

    What proof does He present that there is life after death (vv. 26-27)?

    > **Historical Insight:** Resurrection in the ancient world was understood to be this: physical life after a time of life after death. The Greeks thought it a foolish idea since in their minds anything material (what you could see and touch like bodies) was evil. So why would anyone want to have another body? However, God created the human body as something good. The cross (crucified Messiah) was a stumbling block to the Jews, and the resurrection was foolishness to the Gentiles. But God's plan represents the power of God and the wisdom of God (1 Corinthians 1:24) to all those who believe.

11. **Heartbreak to Hope:** In His answer to the Sadducees (v. 24), Jesus pointed out their illiteracy of the Scriptures and their disregard for the power of God. This is a common occurrence today as well. Do you know people who are going through pain and heartache but refuse to look to the Word of God and the power of God for answers? Why do you think they resist the truth so much? How can you specifically pray for them?

Respond to the Lord about what He's shown you today.

LESSON 8

Day Four Study

Ask the Lord Jesus to speak to you through His Word. Tell Him that you are listening.

Read Mark 12:28-34.

12. ***Discover the Facts***: Here comes Test #4, But this time it is from someone who seems to be sincerely asking the question.

    A teacher of the law (religious lawyer) comes to Jesus and hears the previous debate. What is his test question (v. 28)?

    Jesus starts with the Jewish basic declaration about their God from Deuteronomy 6:4-5. Write Jesus' answer from vv. 30-31 in the space below.

    What is the lawyer's response to this (vv. 32-33)?

    What encouragement does Jesus give to the man (v. 34)?

    From then on, what happened?

    Focus on the Meaning: The lawyer showed he had faith. Most of the religious leaders had degenerated from a personal relationship with God to outward practice of religion without heart. God wants your heart—the seat of your affections.

13. ***Heartbreak to Hope:*** Loving your neighbor as yourself means going beyond the minimum standard of just being nice to someone. Jesus demonstrated going the extra step to love those around you. Example: when someone annoys you, the minimum would be not bad-mouthing that person. The heart of Jesus would lead you to find something kind to say to that person. Think of other examples from your life where you could go beyond the minimum to "love your neighbor as yourself."

HEARTBREAK TO HOPE: GOOD NEWS FROM MARK

Read Mark 12:35-40.

14. *Discover the Facts*: Jesus issues the next test while He is teaching the crowds.

   What is His question (v. 35)?

   Jesus quotes from what is called a Messianic psalm because it references the Messiah. Who wrote the psalm, and who gave him the words to write (v. 36)?

   Write Psalm 110:1 (quoted by Jesus in Mark 12:36) in the space below. This Old Testament verse is the most quoted verse in the New Testament (Matthew 22:43-45; Mark 12:35-37; Luke 20:41-44; Acts 2:33-36; Hebrews 1:13 plus other partial quotes).

   How does the crowd respond?

   What warning does He give next and why (vv. 38-40)?

15. What is the answer to Jesus' question in v. 37? See also Romans 1:1-4 and Colossians 2:9.

16. In what ways are the teachers of the law opposite of Jesus' description of servant leaders in Mark 10:43-45?

96

LESSON 8

Read Mark 12:41-44.

17. ***Discover the Facts***: Jesus was continually "people watching" and teaching His disciples about people. In this section, He presents a contrast to His disciples of someone representing the heart for God that the teachers of the law lacked.

    Where are they?

    What do they see in v. 41?

    What do they see in v. 42?

    What did Jesus see in her heart attitude that He wanted His disciples to grasp (vv. 43-44)?

18. ***Heartbreak to Hope:*** What is your take-away from this lesson that you will apply to your own life?

Respond to the Lord about what He's shown you today.

Recommended: Listen to the podcast "The God You Can Know and Love" after doing this lesson to reinforce what you have learned. Use the following listener guide.

PODCAST LISTENER GUIDE

The God You Can Know and Love

"Love the Lord your God with all your heart and with all your soul and with all your mind and with all your strength." (Mark 12:31)

WHAT IS THEOLOGY?

- Theology is simply what you believe about God. All women are theologians. And it matters if we are good ones or not.

- You have influence. So understanding the truth about God and being able to communicate that truth in casual conversation and serious discussion is one of your greatest assets for any relationship.

- We learn theology like we learn most anything else in life—prepare by instruction, learn by experience. Prepare by instruction means studying the truths about God in the Bible. Learn by experience means to trust in what you have learned about God as you live out your life.

- It's as we study the truth about God in the Bible then trust Him as we live our lives that we learn true theology. You and I can face any impossible situation if we are prepared by instruction about God and teachable to learn through experience with God.

THE GOD YOU CAN KNOW

- We can know the truth about God by what are called His attributes. An "attribute" is a quality or characteristic of someone or something.

- The attributes of God are things we can know about God. They describe His character and are true about Him all the time. God's greatness is far beyond human understanding. But God has revealed enough about Himself in His Word so we can know who He is.

GOD'S ATTRIBUTES REVEAL HIS CHARACTER.

So let's consider a few of the attributes of God and how each one affects your view of God and your relationship with Him.

- God's **sovereignty**. God is the sovereign ruler over His creation. He rules it with supreme authority and power. *2 Samuel 7:22*

- God's **holiness**. God is set apart from anything that is sinful or evil. *Habakkuk 1:13a*

- God's **omnipresence, omnipotence,** and **omniscience.** *Psalm 139:5-6 NIRV*
    - ✓ God's omnipresence: God is present everywhere at the same time.
    - ✓ God's omnipotence: God is all powerful, more powerful than anything or anyone else in the entire universe.
    - ✓ God's omniscience: God is all knowing. He knows everything there is to know.

- God's **love**. God's love is patient, kind, forgiving and considers what is best for the one being loved. *Psalm 103:8*

- God's **goodness**. God is good all the time. He is good in the tough times, in different ways for each person, and in what He allows or does not allow into our lives. *Psalm 119:68*

GOD IS TRUSTWORTHY OF YOUR LOVE.

- Trust (faith) is always an issue of credibility. Knowing God's character plus His promises gives you plenty of reasons to consider Him trustworthy.

- God is also a trustworthy Father. The moment you placed your trust in Jesus Christ for your salvation, you were adopted into God's family as His child. He is the perfect Father, the most loving Father, the most dependable Father, and the Father who cares about your every need. You are dearly loved by your Father God.

KNOWING THE TRUTH ABOUT GOD LEADS TO FOLLOWING JESUS.

- What Jesus did and said in His earthly life was an unmistakable demonstration of God to the people of Jesus' day.

- The cross followed by the resurrection is the single most important event in human history and a demonstration of God's attributes. There is only one way to the true God—by faith in His Son Jesus Christ. That's His plan.

- Christianity is Christ! It's not a lifestyle or rules of conduct. It's not a society whose members were initiated by the sprinkling or covering of water. We are called first and foremost to a relationship with a **Person—Jesus Christ**.

   God's plan for your life is simple: Follow His Son. But you won't follow someone you don't trust. You can't trust someone you don't know, and you cannot know Christ apart from His Word. (Rebecca Carrell, heartstrongfaith.com)

- We must see Him through eyes of faith and allow the gospels to leap off the page revealing our Lord.

- Through seeing Jesus in the pages of the gospels, we get to see who God is because Jesus has the attributes of God—the very same ones.

- Women need good theology so we don't get caught sitting on the fence like some of the people of Jesus' day did. And if we have good theology about our God, then we won't do harm when family and friends depend on us for counsel.

Let Jesus satisfy your heart with hope, healing, and love as you get to know Him and trust Him more each day.

Lesson 9: Prophecy, Perfume and Passover

(Mark 13:1-14:42)

Day One Study

Ask the Lord Jesus to speak to you through His Word. Tell Him that you are listening.

Read Mark 13:1-37.

The disciples get a glimpse of the future, beyond the cross and grave that Jesus was already telling them to expect. We'll cover this sermon of Jesus in 5 parts. We may not know the when and the how. But there are specific things we can know. At the end of each section, we'll focus on what those are.

1. **Discover the Facts, Part 1**: Focus on vv. 1-8.

    The disciples commented on the massive stones and magnificence of the Temple. What did Jesus say to them (v. 2)? Note: this destruction took place in 70 AD.

    As they were sitting on the Mount of Olives, what did Andrew ask Jesus?

    What warning did Jesus give them (v. 5)?

    Summarize what Jesus said in vv. 6-8.

What We Can Know #1: Conditions on this planet are not going to get better but worse! We can forget about the idea of world peace until Jesus comes back.

2. **Discover the Facts, Part 2:** Focus on vv. 9-13.

    What will happen to Jesus' disciples (v. 9)?

What must happen before the end comes (v. 10)?

> **Scriptural Insight:** This is the responsibility of every generation of disciples (Matt. 28:19). "Must" (Gr. *dei*) indicates divine necessity. God wants this to happen, and it will happen. This verse is not a promise that if disciples will preach the gospel to all nations in a particular generation, God will then begin the kingdom. Man cannot bring in the kingdom by the universal preaching of the gospel. God will bring it in at His appointed time. This is not a promise that everyone will become a believer in Jesus, either. (*Dr. Constable's Notes on Mark 2017 Edition*, p. 189)

What are they not to do when they are arrested and why (v. 11)?

What is the warning in vv. 12-13?

> **From the Greek:** "Saved" in v. 13 comes from the Greek word *sozo*, meaning "to be kept safe, to rescue from danger or destruction." Rescue comes from the persecution ending, by death, or by Jesus' second coming. This is not a salvation verse; it is an encouragement to persevere.

What We Can Know #2: *Persecutions and betrayals will affect Christians until Jesus returns. He'll give us strength to endure them plus words to say, and we are not to live in fear.*

3. **Discover the Facts, Part 3:** Focus on vv. 14-23.

    Mark skips over the destruction of Jerusalem that Matthew and Luke include. That was a taste of future desolation. Read Luke 21:24. We are in the "until" time, "**until** the times of the Gentiles are fulfilled." Jesus finally answers their question from v. 4.

    What is the one sign they will see and recognize? See also Daniel 9:25-27.

    What are they to do when that happens (vv. 14-16)?

    On whom will this time be especially hard and why (vv. 17-18)?

What did Jesus say about this calamity (v. 19)?

> **Think About It:** Since WWII was worse than the destruction of Jerusalem in 70 A.D., we know that this tribulation hasn't happened yet.

Why has God limited that awful time of Tribulation to just 7 years (we learn this from Daniel and Revelation also)?

What can happen to Christians during that time of distress and waiting (vv. 21-22)?

So what should you do to protect yourself (v. 23)?

What We Can Know #3: *This great time of worldwide massive tribulation hasn't happened yet. The destruction of Jerusalem was not the worst that had happened before or even since that time. It is still to come.*

Respond to the Lord about what He's shown you today.

Day Two Study

Ask the Lord Jesus to speak to you through His Word. Tell Him that you are listening.

Read Mark 13:24-37.

We will continue to cover this sermon of Jesus.

4. ***Discover the Facts, Part 4:*** Focus on vv. 24-31.

    Following that distress, what signs will show in the heavens (vv. 24-25)?

    At that time, what will everyone on earth see (v. 26)? See also Mark 8:38.

What is promised in v. 27 to give us comfort?

What is the lesson of the fig tree (vv. 28-29)?

What is the promise in vv. 30-31?

What We Can Know #4: *Jesus is physically coming back to planet Earth, and no one is going to miss it this time. We just don't know when. What does Jesus mean by "this generation?" It could be the Jews. It is probably not a number of years. Luke 21:24 tells us that the Jews will be scattered worldwide at that time.*

5. **Discover the Facts, Part 5:** Focus on vv. 32-37.

    Who determines the time for the Tribulation and the Second Coming (v. 32)?

    Can we figure it out (v. 33)?

    What can we do or should we do while waiting?

    Why stay alert?

    What is the job of the door keeper in the parable Jesus told in vv. 34-37?

What We Can Know #5: *Jesus leaves His disciples here with certain responsibilities. To them and to all of us, He says, "Stay alert. Watch out that no one deceives you. Be doing my work daily."*

6. Many people missed Jesus' first coming. Will anyone alive miss Jesus' second coming? Even if asleep? How do we know? Give verses from this sermon.

7. The word translated "watch out" means "to see and discern." Jesus tells them to watch out for deception several times in this sermon (Mark 13:9, 23, 33, 35, and 37). What is the danger of deception?

   Think About It: A disciple's greatest danger is not war, not calamity, not persecution, or even betrayal. It is DECEPTION. Deception affects the direction our minds are going and where our bodies follow.

8. ***Heartbreak to Hope:*** You are to "watch out that no one deceives you" from following Christ. What are you tempted to follow more than Christ?

Respond to the Lord about what He's shown you today.

Day Three Study

Ask the Lord Jesus to speak to you through His Word. Tell Him that you are listening.

Read Mark 14:1-11 and John 12:1-11.

9. ***Discover the Facts***: The religious leaders were scheming to arrest Jesus secretly and kill him. But not during the festival. Jesus was spending time with His friends Martha, Mary, and Lazarus. Something beautiful happens.

   Where were they (v. 3)?

   What did Mary do (v. 3)?

What was the disciples' emotional reaction and why (vv. 4-5)? See also John 12:4-6.

Look at Jesus' response to them (vv. 6-9). What did He say about her to His disciples?

What happened next (vv. 10-11?

10. What did Jesus mean by "she did what she could" (v. 8)?

11. **Heartbreak to Hope:** The same thing that Jesus said about Mary is true for you. Think about your daily work where you are using your resources, God-given temperament, opportunity and love to honor and worship Jesus. In what ways can it be said of you, "She did what she could?"

Read Mark 14:12-26.

12. **Discover the Facts**: Jesus introduces to His disciples a way to remember His sacrifice in what is called "The Lord's Supper." We know it as communion. It is the preparation day for the Passover. The disciples asked what Jesus wanted them to do.

    What are Jesus' directions to them (vv. 13-15)?

    That evening, how did Jesus shock the Twelve (v. 18)?

    What is their response (v. 19)?

    What does Jesus declare next (vv. 20-21)?

Think About It: John 13:27 says that Satan entered Judas who then left. Jesus warned him but that didn't stop him. Throughout the Bible, God warns people of their actions before they take them. That's His love and grace. Yet, many ignore His warning.

What did Jesus do in vv. 22-23?

What does He say about drinking from the cup? See also Jeremiah 31:31-34.

What does He promise them (v. 25)?

Most of John 13-17 takes place between v. 25 and v. 26. What did they do afterwards (v. 26)?

Think About It: Each of the disciples thought he was capable of betrayal (v. 19). The world is full of betrayers. Betrayal will happen, but woe to the one who allowed himself to be used.

13. **Heartbreak to Hope:** Have you been betrayed by a friend? Read Hebrews 4:15-16. Jesus understands how you feel about betrayal and everything else you experience in life. Pour out your heart to Him. Ask Him for help to overcome the hurt you feel and wisdom to know what to do about that relationship.

Scriptural Insight: Although Jesus Christ is now in a glorified human body in Heaven, He is with us by means of the Holy Spirit. The Holy Spirit is *"God's Empowering Presence"* in our lives. That is what He is and does. He enables us to feel God's love for us, and He fills us with hope that God is at work within us and for us according to His promises. When we are weak, He carries our prayer needs directly to God the Father or God the Son and then works in our lives according to what is needed for us. At times of crisis, we can have confidence that our God both hears our need and is acting upon it on our behalf.

Respond to the Lord about what He's shown you today.

Day Four Study

Ask the Lord Jesus to speak to you through His Word. Tell Him that you are listening.

Read Mark 14:27-31.

14. ***Discover the Facts:*** Jesus shares words of caution to His disciples.

    What does Jesus tell them (v. 27)?

    After that, what will happen (v. 28)?

    What does Peter declare (v. 29?

    How does Jesus answer him (v. 30)?

    What is Peter's emphatic response (v. 31)?

    Was he alone in saying this?

15. Read Luke 22:31-32. How did Jesus pray for Peter?

Read Mark 14:32-42.

16. ***Discover the Facts:*** Jesus understands how we feel when we're about to face something awful. He's been there.

    As they were heading to Gethsemane, what did Jesus say to them (v. 32)?

As Jesus took Peter, James, and John with Him to pray, how is He feeling (vv. 33-34)?

Then, what does He ask them to do?

As Jesus fell to the ground to pray, what did He see to His Father (vv. 35-36)?

Focus on the Meaning: "Abba Father" is expressive of an especially close relationship to God. It is informal and intimate, similar to saying, "Daddy." We can call God "Abba Father," also. See Romans 8:15 and Galatians 4:6.

What does He find when He returns to the disciples (v. 37)?

How does Jesus warn Peter again (v. 38)?

Read Luke 22:43-44. What was happening to Jesus during this third time of prayer?

What does Jesus declare to His disciples in Mark 14:41-42?

Think About It: The words of Mark 14:42 are words of courage. Through prayer and God's strengthening, Jesus is prepared for the battle ahead. He chose God's will, which included suffering. No Christian ever chooses suffering. She should choose God's will, as Jesus did, whether it means suffering or not.

17. **Heartbreak to Hope:** Peter, like the rest of the disciples, made a vow of good intentions. Good intentions are just that—intentions—until you make them intentional actions. Our natural humanity cannot follow up on good intentions. We must pray and trust in Jesus to help us turn good intentions into intentional actions.

    - What good intentions have you promised or planned to do but have not followed up with intentional actions?

- What will you trust Jesus to do in your life to help you carry through with at least one of those good intentions?

18. **Heartbreak to Hope:** Reflect back on this whole lesson, how did someone experiencing heartbreak, pain, or uncertainty find hope, healing and love?

Respond to the Lord about what He's shown you today.

Recommended: Listen to the podcast "Avoiding Deception Trails" after doing this lesson to reinforce what you have learned. Use the following listener guide.

PODCAST LISTENER GUIDE

Avoiding Deception Trails

From Mark chapter 13, there are 5 things we can know for sure.

- *What We Can Know #1 (vv. 7-8):* Jesus said conditions on this planet are not going to get better but worse! We can forget the idea of world peace until He comes back.

- *What We Can Know #2 (vv. 9-13):* Persecutions and betrayals will affect Christians until Jesus returns. He will give us strength to endure them plus the words to say. And we are not to be afraid.

- *What We Can Know #3 (vv. 14-23):* This great time of worldwide, massive tribulation hasn't happened yet. The destruction of Jerusalem in 70 AD was not the worst that had happened before that or even since that time. It is still to come.

- *What We Can Know #4 (vv. 24-27):* Jesus is physically coming back to planet Earth, and no one is going to miss it. Isn't that good news? We just don't know when He is returning.

- *What We Can Know #5 (vv. 33-37):* Jesus is leaving His disciples behind with certain responsibilities. To them and to all of us, He says, "Stay alert."

- In Mark 13, Jesus warned that a disciple's greatest danger is not war, calamity, persecution, or betrayal. It is deception.

WATCH OUT THAT NO ONE DECEIVES YOU.

- Deception affects the direction our minds are going and our bodies follow. The further we get into the last days and the more complex society gets, the easier it is to be deceived.

- Our Bible is like a map that gives us an aerial view of the right trail following Jesus as well as all the wrong ones. And the Holy Spirit is our compass, always orienting us to Jesus and His way. Without relying on our map and compass, we can easily be deceived. *2 Corinthians 11:3*

- We have a spiritual enemy, and deceiving us is one of his best means for making us ineffective at pursuing Christ completely. We put all our energy going in the wrong directions. Let's call those deception trails.

- Deception trails are anything that wastes our time, energy and money by sending us in a direction away from our responsibilities as a disciple that Jesus mentioned in Mark 13. These are knowing Christ and following Him only plus being His witnesses as we let Him live His life through us. When we choose to make certain mistakes, we become vulnerable to deception trails.

DECEPTION TRAIL #1 IS TO IGNORE THE MAP AND COMPASS AND GO BY HOW YOU FEEL.

- Emotions can distract us because they are responders. They will line up with anything we want them to match. Relying on how we feel about something rather than on the Bible and the Holy Spirit to guide us makes us vulnerable to being deceived.

- Trust the Holy Spirit to help you find a New Testament verse that teaches truth about any issue. Then, let your emotions respond to God's Word.

DECEPTION TRAIL #2 IS THINKING GREAT GEAR AND A GREAT BODY GUARANTEE A GREAT HIKE.

- Hikers in perfect physical shape with very expensive boots and equipment still get blisters on the trail and altitude sickness. Having a nicer home, newer car, or stylish clothes and a better body will not make us happier.

- The more serious deception is that pleasing our physical senses should take priority in our lives so we will be strong enough to get through life. We need to predetermine what will take priority before we're bombarded with others' demands. Or the lesser things will dominate. We can ask Jesus to help us prioritize our lives because He shows us how.

DECEPTION TRAIL #3 IS TO ASSUME ALL SIGNPOSTS ARE ACCURATE.

- Jesus warned His disciples twice in Mark 13 about listening to other voices instead of His voice. What tricks is our culture doing to influence our thinking? And how does our response affect those around us?

- Some cultural signposts are misleading, maybe even rotten at the bottom. They keep us from being effective at following Jesus.

- Paul warned about a time when people will not put up with sound doctrine but will gather around them teachers what say what their itching ears want to hear. *2 Timothy 4:3-4*

- Ask Jesus to help you be a good doorkeeper of your mind and mouth. Compare what you are being told with what God's Word says. *Colossians 2:8*

- An important trail rule is for hikers in a group to stay within sight and sound of the leader. As believers, we need to stay within sight and sound of Jesus' voice, which are the Bible and the Holy Spirit within us. When we don't, we make ourselves vulnerable to following a deception trail.

- What changes do you need to make today to keep you alert to deceptions and to rely on your map and compass so that you can hike Jesus' trail effectively?

Let Jesus satisfy your heart with hope, healing, and love as you get to know Him and trust Him more each day.

Lesson 10: Facing the Giants

(Mark 14:43-15:47)

Question to consider: Recall the worst 12 hours of your life. What happened? How did you get through it?

Historical Insight: Here is a possible timeline for the day of the crucifixion.

3 AM	4-6 AM	6-8 AM	9 AM	Noon to 3 PM	3 PM
Arrest	Trial before the High Priest and the Sanhedrin	Trial before Pilate	Crucified	Darkness over the land	Jesus died

DAY ONE STUDY

Ask the Lord Jesus to speak to you through His Word. Tell Him that you are listening.

Read Mark 14:43-52.

1. ***Discover the Facts***: Jesus was praying and waiting in the garden to be arrested. He knew it would happen; this was not a surprise to God. Jesus did not run away.

   The Sanhedrin sent a crowd armed with swords and clubs to arrest Jesus. How did they identify Him (vv. 44-45)?

   How did you feel when you read that Judas called Jesus "rabbi" and kissed Him?

   What did the disciple standing nearby do to defend Jesus (vv. 46-47)? See John 18:10.

   What is Jesus' response to the crowd, exposing their deceitfulness (vv. 48-49)?

   What happened to His disciples (v. 50)? But see v. 54.

   Who else was there as an eyewitness (vv. 51-52)?

Did God need a betrayer for Jesus to get arrested? No. He chose to use Judas's sinfulness to represent the sin of man in opposition against God. Judas represented evil, the sinfulness of man. And Judas was part of God's plan to fulfill the Scriptures in Isaiah 53 and Psalm 22.

Read Mark 14:53-65.

2. ***Discover the Facts***: Not all of the 70 members of the Sanhedrin were present at this "trial." Jesus was taken to the house of the high priest. Peter followed at a distance and sat with the guards in the courtyard.

   What did the religious leaders want but could not get (vv. 55-56)?

   What was the accusation against Him (vv. 57-59)?

   > **Scriptural Insight:** There is no recorded statement from Jesus about this. Perhaps it is a misuse of His words in John 2:18-22. In Acts 7, we read that the Sanhedrin throws a similar accusation at Stephen and stones him for it.

   Jesus refused to respond to their accusations (vv. 60-61). But, when asked if He is the Christ, the Son of the Blessed One, what did Jesus say (v. 62)?

   What was the High Priest's response (vv. 63-64)?

   > **Focus on the Meaning:** Remember that blasphemy is anything that slanders God's name or claims God's majesty and authority. Jesus did not commit blasphemy since He was the Son of God as He said.

   What did the onlookers do (vv. 64-65)?

3. Read v. 62 again. Read Psalm 110:1 and Daniel 7:13-14. Did Jesus claim to be the Messiah, the Son of God?

LESSON 10

4. ***Heartbreak to Hope***: What in today's study speaks to your heart?

Respond to the Lord about what He's shown you today.

Day Two Study

Ask the Lord Jesus to speak to you through His Word. Tell Him that you are listening.

Read Mark 14:66-72.

5. ***Discover the Facts***: While Jesus was being attacked upstairs, Peter was being attacked in a different way.

    A servant girl came by Peter in the courtyard and identified Peter as one of those who were with Jesus. How did Peter answer (v. 68)?

    Though the servant girl insisted Peter was one of the Galileans who had been with Jesus, what is Peter's response twice more (v. 71)?

    What did Peter remember when he heard the rooster crow (v. 72)?

    > **Think About It:** As I was preparing this lesson, I realized that Peter wanted to stay close by because he loved Jesus. And he wanted to just be left alone. It wasn't his faith that failed him. It was his courage and maybe his hope. Add to that exhaustion. How often does exhaustion, wanting to be left alone, and avoiding conflict get you into trouble?

6. ***Heartbreak to Hope:*** God doesn't entice anyone to sin (James 1:13-14), but He does lead us to a place where we are tested (Job 1; Matthew 4:1; 6:13). His method of instruction is 1) Prepare by instruction (what Jesus had done) and 2) Learn by experience.

    Testing reveals to us that we are weak in our humanity regarding even our good intentions. It also shows the terrible possibilities in us because sin is still in us. But testing teaches us that the safest place to be is in humble dependence upon God (Romans 13:14; 2 Corinthians 1:9). Our prayer should be, "Lord, protect me from myself." What have you learned through a time of testing?

HEARTBREAK TO HOPE: GOOD NEWS FROM MARK

Read Mark 15:1-15.

7. ***Discover the Facts***: Pilate was a bad dude. He minted coins with pagan images on them. He stole from the temple treasury to build an aqueduct and killed those who protested against that. Pilate represents worldly authority.

   Historical Insight: The Sanhedrin apparently reached the decision to accuse Jesus before the civil authority for treason rather than blasphemy. Then He could be executed by the Romans. (*NIV Study Bible 1984 Edition*, note on Mark 15:1, p. 1527)

   The Sanhedrin bound Jesus, led him away, and handed him over to Pilate. What did Pilate ask Jesus (v. 2)?

   How did Jesus answer Pilate?

   After hearing the Jews accuse Jesus of many things, what is Pilate's next question (v. 4)?

   When Jesus refused to answer, what is Pilate's response (v. 5)?

   Historical Insight: According to Roman Law, if the accused made no defense, he would be considered guilty and judged as guilty.

   Pilate could release Jesus or the murderous rebel in his jail. What did he recognize in the religious leaders (v. 10)?

   The religious leaders stirred up the crowds to have Barabbas released. When Pilate questioned the crowd, what answers did they give to Pilate that convinced him to release Barabbas (vv. 12-14)?

   Think About It: Was Pilate acting as an impartial judge? No. He asked questions for which he didn't really want answers. His judicial decision was prompted by a desire to satisfy the crowd. Judgment in a Roman court was the sole responsibility of the imperial magistrate. There was no jury of peers. Pilate was a man of the world who rationalized to evade responsibility and the truth. Interestingly, he wanted to wash himself of blame for

LESSON 10

this judgment, but every doctrinal creed for Christians since this day says, "Suffered under Pontius Pilate." God didn't let him be forgotten.

8. ***Heartbreak to Hope***: What in today's study speaks to your heart?

Respond to the Lord about what He's shown you today.

Day Three Study

Ask the Lord Jesus to speak to you through His Word. Tell Him that you are listening.

Read Mark 15:16-20.

9. ***Discover the Facts***: Before this time, Jesus had little interaction with Roman soldiers (who were all non-Jewish) except for those centurions who sought His help in healing someone from their household.

Where did the soldiers take Jesus (v. 16)?

What did they do and say to Him there (vv. 17-19)?

After they finished mocking Jesus, what did they do (v. 20)?

Read Mark 15:21-32.

> **Historical Insight:** Crucifixion as a means of execution had been around for at least 100 years. The Phoenicians used it. Even a Jewish king had used it. The Romans popularized it, primarily using it for revolutionaries, criminals, and slaves to deter rebellion. To keep the Jews satisfied, they did not leave crucified Jews on the cross after death though non-Jews were left for days. Roman citizens were never crucified. Jesus was identified with the lowest of society here.

10. ***Discover the Facts:*** Mark's account of the crucifixion is the briefest of the four gospels. You can read Matthew 27:33-34; Luke 23:33-43; and John 19:17-24 to find out more information.

> **Scriptural Insight:** Simon was probably a Jew who was in Jerusalem to celebrate the Passover. Alexander and Rufus are only mentioned by Mark, but referred to in such a way as to suggest that they were known by those to whom he wrote. Rufus may be the same person spoken of by Paul in Romans 16:13. (*NIV Study Bible 1984 Edition,* note on Mark 15:21, p. 1528)

Where did they take Jesus (v. 22)?

What happened there (vv. 23-24)?

> **Historical Insight:** It was the accepted right of the executioner's squad to claim the minor possessions of the victim. Jesus' clothing likely consisted of an under and an outer garment, a belt, sandals and possibly a head covering. Casting lots was a common practice for them to do this and fulfilled Psalm 22:18. (*NIV Study Bible 1984 Edition,* note on Mark 15:24, p. 1529)

What did the sign above his head say (v. 26)?

Who else was crucified that day (v. 27)?

What did those passing by do (vv. 29-30)?

What did the chief priests and lawyers do and admit about Him (vv. 31-32)?

11. Were the religious leaders sincere in their statement that they would believe if He came down from the cross? How do you know?

12. Read Luke 23:40-43. What do we know about one of those who were crucified with Jesus?

Think About It: Sin was very ugly that day. The one who was supposed to represent Jesus before God—the chief priest—did not do that. Those guiltier than Jesus heaped insults on Him. Those who saw Jesus heal many ("save others") felt no compassion for His unjust execution. But this was all part of God's plan. There were no surprises.

13. *Heartbreak to Hope*: What in today's study speaks to your heart?

Respond to the Lord about what He's shown you today.

Day Four Study

Ask the Lord Jesus to speak to you through His Word. Tell Him that you are listening.

Read Mark 15:33-41.

14. *Discover the Facts*: Jesus spoke 7 times from the cross. Mark only records 1 of them. What happened between noon and 3 PM (v. 33)?

Historical Insight: Based on the latest research into historical records, it is generally thought that the Crucifixion took place on Friday, April 3, A.D. 33 and the resurrection on Sunday, April 5. The Crucifixion had to occur in a year when Nisan 14 fell on a Friday. This happened in A.D. 33. Astronomy presents another insight related to the Crucifixion. Just as the sun was setting on April 3 of A.D. 33, there was an eclipse of the moon, giving the moon a dark red color. (Rodger C. Young, *Book review: From Abraham to Paul: A Biblical Chronology*, by Andrew E. Steinmann, accessed online)

Read Amos 8:9-10 for the prediction of this event. What are the similarities?

At 3 PM, what did Jesus cry out (v. 34)?

Think About It: Why did Jesus quote Psalm 22:1? The words accurately reflect what Jesus felt in His humanity, just as He shrunk back from the cross while in the garden. He identified with people in the horror of sin as the sin of the world was placed on Him. But He was in the center of God's will for His life and not really forsaken by God. Perhaps He was pointing those listening to Psalm 22, whose words amazingly describe a crucifixion 1000 years before this happened. It was as if He was saying, "David wrote about me." Although often taught that God turned His back on Jesus that day, there is no verse in the New Testament declaring that. It is a mystery beyond our comprehension regarding what was going on between the Father and the Son at the cross.

What did the bystanders hear and do (vv. 35-36)?

How did Jesus die (v. 37)? See John 19:30.

What happened next (v. 38)? See also Matthew 27:51.

Historical Insight: The inner "veil" of the temple is probably in view here, the one separating the holy place from the most holy place. It was a most elaborately woven fabric that was 60 feet high, 30 feet wide, and of the thickness of the palm of the hand. The tearing happened at 3:00 PM, the time of the evening incense offering. A priest would normally have been standing in the holy place offering incense when it tore (cf. Luke 1:8-10). Some early non-biblical Jewish sources also report unusual phenomena in the temple 40 years before its destruction in A.D. 70, one of which is the temple curtain tearing. The fact that this occurred from top to bottom signified that God is the One who ripped the thick curtain. It was not torn from the bottom by men ripping it. (*Dr. Constable's Notes on Matthew 2017 Edition*, p. 471)

Based on the above information, what does the tearing from top to bottom mean?

What did the Roman centurion notice and declare (v. 39)?

Who else was there watching (vv. 40-41)?

Think About It: Many of these women had been caring for His needs for a long time. But now God is in charge, and they aren't. They probably felt helpless since they could do nothing for Him. Jesus told them the plan too. Like the men, they didn't get it. So they might have felt hopeless as well.

If you trace the use of the words "follow" and "minister" throughout the Gospel of Mark, you will see how the author used these same words to depict serious disciples. ... The women as depicted by Mark do "whatever disciples may do on behalf of their teachers," which might include table service, but it may include other forms of self-denying sacrifice, as well.

15. "It is finished" (John 19:30). These final words from Jesus come from an accounting term in Greek meaning, "a debt is paid in full." What debt was paid in full that day? See Colossians 2:13-14 and other Bible verses you know that answer this question.

Think About It: When Jesus said, "It is finished." God agreed. It is finished. The debt for sin was paid in full. The Old Covenant represented by the veil separating man from God is over. The New Covenant began.

Read Mark 15:42-47.

16. ***Discover the Facts***: Jesus' friends couldn't help during the crucifixion. But now they can do something to show their love for Him.

    What was coming soon that created the urgency to act (v. 42)?

    What is known about the one who buried Jesus' body (v. 43)? See also Matthew 27:57.

    What actions did Pilate take in response to Joseph's request (vv. 44-45)?

    What did Joseph do (v. 46)? See who helped him in John 19:39.

    What did Mary Magdalene and Mary the mother of Joses see (v. 47)?

Historical Insight: The Romans confirmed that Jesus was truly dead and had not just swooned or passed out. Two women knew exactly where the body was placed and would not have forgotten that location between Friday and Sunday.

17. ***Heartbreak to Hope:*** Ugly sin nailed sinless Jesus to a shameful cross in our place. Yet, our God is able to make ugly beautiful. What ugliness in your life has God made beautiful because of your faith in Jesus' death on the cross for you?

Respond to the Lord about what He's shown you today.

Recommended: Listen to the podcast "God's Grace Makes Ugly Beautiful" after doing this lesson to reinforce what you have learned. Use the following listener guide.

LESSON 10

PODCAST LISTENER GUIDE

God's Grace Makes Ugly Beautiful

Almost 2000 years ago, the beautiful Son of God voluntarily experienced the ugliness of sin and took on its punishment for our sakes.

SIN IS THE FATAL DISEASE.

- Our sinful spiritual condition is like "death caused by a fatal disease." Sin is "the disease," and everyone has it. It's fatal because the result of the sin disease is always death. Our sin separates us from having a relationship with our holy God. That's a spiritual death.

- But God's love for people and His mercy towards us led Him to take action. The Son of God came to earth to live as a human without sin and to offer Himself as a sacrifice for sin once for all. Never again would an animal need to die for human sin. Jesus Christ did that for us on the cross. Crucifixion was ugly. It was a place of agony and disgrace.

PSALM 22 PROPHESIED THE AGONY AND DISGRACE OF CRUCIFIXION

- Psalm 22 prophetically describes the agony that Jesus experienced during His crucifixion.
    - ✓ The crucified victim hung by his outstretched arms attached to the crossbeam. Usually heavy wrought-iron nails were driven through the wrists and the heel bones. *Psalm 22:16*
    - ✓ As the victim hung dangling by the arms, the blood could no longer circulate to his vital organs, and he felt like he was suffocating. His bones would get out of joint. *Psalm 22:14*
    - ✓ The victim would sweat profusely and be thirsty. *Psalm 22:15*
    - ✓ Sometimes wood was nailed to the main post as a sort of seat. Only by supporting himself on this or by pushing against the nails in his feet could the victim lift himself up to gain any relief. Then exhaustion set in, and death followed, although sometimes not for several days.
    - ✓ To hasten death, the victim's legs were broken with a club so he couldn't keep pushing up to stay alive. The fact that Jesus' bones were not broken fulfilled another prophecy from Psalm 22.

- Psalm 22 prophetically describes the disgrace that Jesus experienced during His crucifixion.
    - ✓ The words in Psalm 22:6-8 describe the humiliation of public execution and match what the crowd actually said to Jesus.
    - ✓ The casting of lots seen in Psalm 22:18 was literally fulfilled.

WHY THE CROSS?

- Crucifixion provided the best scenario for Jews and non-Jews alike because both groups participated in the sinful act of executing God's Son. *Acts 2:23*

- It was God's plan for His Son to die on that cross for all of humanity's sin. No human being would ever come up with that plan. It requires faith alone, which is exactly what God wanted. *1 Corinthians 1:23-24*

"Paul persisted in preaching Jesus as the crucified Savior and sin-bearer, the unexpected happened: pagans, as well as Jews and God-fearers, believed the message and found their lives transformed by a new, liberating power, which broke the stranglehold of selfishness and vice and purified them from within. The message of Christ crucified had thus accomplished something which no [amount] of Greek philosophic teaching could have done for them." (F. F. Bruce, *Paul, the Apostle of the Heart Set Free,* p. 253)

- Every bit of our sin is so ugly to God. As ugly as the crucifixion. But our redemption is absolutely beautiful. But God makes ugly beautiful.

THE BEAUTY OF WHAT CHRIST HAS DONE FOR YOU

- Because of Jesus' death on the cross, believers are cleansed of all sin and made new creations of life when God plants His Spirit within us. We are made alive as Christ is alive. That's beautiful. *Colossians 2:13-14*

- God gives us eternal spiritual life from the moment we believe, and we have complete acceptance before a holy God by faith alone. That which stood against us, the ugliness of our sin, is gone. Christ's life is given to us, living in us. That's beautiful.

- When we die, we now have hope of eternal life in the presence of God so physical death is no longer to be feared. Jesus frees us from the fear of death. *Hebrews 2:14-15*

LIVE OUT THE BEAUTIFUL.

- You get to live out this beautiful new life each day. Paul told us how to live this beautiful new life each and every day in Galatians 2 20:

    "I have been crucified with Christ and I no longer live, but Christ lives in me. The life I live in the body, I live by faith in the Son of God, who loved me and gave himself for me." (Gal. 2:20)

- The ugliness of the crucifixion becomes the beauty of Christ's life in you, in me. Are you grateful for the beauty that God has made out of your ugliness? Are you longing to worship Him for it?

- What ugliness in your life has God made beautiful because of Jesus Christ living in you? Let your heart sing out to Him joyfully today and every day. Graceful living starts with God making ugly beautiful in your life.

Let Jesus satisfy your heart with hope, healing, and love as you get to know Him and trust Him more each day.

Lesson 11: He Is Alive! Hope Springs New

(Mark 16:1-8; Matthew 27:62-28:20; Luke 24:1-35; John 20:1-31)

DAY ONE STUDY

Ask the Lord Jesus to speak to you through His Word. Tell Him that you are listening.

Read Matthew 27:62-66.

1. *Discover the Facts:* The religious leaders weren't satisfied with just having Jesus crucified.

    On Saturday, while Jesus was dead in the tomb, what did the religious leaders ask Pilate to do (vv. 62-64)?

    What happened then (vv. 65-66)?

    Focus on the Meaning: Jesus' first "deception" from their viewpoint was His messiahship, and His "last" (second) was His claim that He would rise from the dead. The falsely pious chief priests and Pharisees pretended to want to protect the people from deception. Matthew viewed their action as self-deception designed to deceive others ("blind leading the blind"). ... *they* were the real deceivers of the people. (*Dr. Constable's Notes on Matthew 2017 Edition*, p. 477)

Read Mark 16:1-8.

2. *Discover the Facts:* Now, we get to look at the greatest miracle in human history.

    What did the 3 women do after sunset on Saturday (v. 1)?

    What were they not expecting to happen?

    What was their concern as they headed to the tomb early Sunday morning (vv. 2-3)?

    When they got there, what did they see (v. 4)?

As they entered the tomb, what did they see and not see (v. 5)?

What was their response?

What did the young man (Matthew and John identify him as an angel) tell them not to do?

After confirming their intent to find Jesus, what did he say to them?

What instruction did the angel give to the women (v. 7)?

According to Luke 24:6-8, what did they remember?

What was Jesus' plan for meeting with His followers?

How did the women feel then (v. 8)?

What did they do even though feeling that way?

Scriptural Insight: Verses 9-20 are not original to Mark. The earliest and best manuscripts do not have them. Most scholars believe they were added later. The word choice and writing style are different from Mark's style. We don't have any record of Jesus giving His disciples authority to pick up snakes or drink poison. Everything else is a summary of what is found in the other gospels. So either Mark ended his book at v. 8 or the rest of it was lost. Because of word choices in v. 8, many scholars think that Mark wrote more and did not intend to end at v. 8.

3. ***Heartbreak to Hope:*** What in today's study speaks to your heart?

Respond to the Lord about what He's shown you today.

Day Two Study

Ask the Lord Jesus to speak to you through His Word. Tell Him that you are listening.

Read Matthew 28:1-10.

4. ***Discover the Facts:*** We will learn a few more details from Matthew's account of Resurrection Sunday.

   According to v. 2, what had just happened?

   Focus on the Meaning: Only Matthew mentions the earthquakes that happened at Jesus' death and at His resurrection. These were significant signs for the Jews. Matthew wrote his gospel primarily for those who were Jewish.

   What was the angel's appearance like (v. 3)?

   How did the guards respond to this event (v. 4)?

   Scriptural Insight: All of these events have supernatural connotations. An angel had announced the Incarnation, and now an angel announced the Resurrection (1:20-23; cf. 18:10). The angel rolled the stone away to admit the witnesses, not to allow Jesus to escape (cf. John 20:26). The guards experienced the earthquake and observed the angel, who appeared as a young man (Mark 16:5). It was seeing the angel—whose appearance was also "like lightning," which evidently terrified them so greatly—that Matthew could describe them as appearing "like dead men" (vv. 3-4). Perhaps they fainted "dead away," as in a deep sleep or coma. (*Dr. Constable's Notes on Matthew 2017 Edition*, p. 478)

   What is added in v. 8 to what Mark wrote about the women leaving the tomb?

Who met them on the way, and what did He say to them (v. 9)?

What did the women do?

What did Jesus tell them not to do (v. 10)?

What were they to do?

What new relationship does Jesus now have with the disciples?

Read Matthew 28:11-15.

5. **Discover the Facts:** The guards reported what had happened to the chief priests. The religious leaders had to come up with a "Plan B."

    What deceptive plan did the chief priests and elders make (vv. 12-15)?

    Did it work?

6. **Heartbreak to Hope:** What in today's study speaks to your heart?

Respond to the Lord about what He's shown you today.

LESSON 11

DAY THREE STUDY

Ask the Lord Jesus to speak to you through His Word. Tell Him that you are listening.

Read John 20:1-18.

7. ***Discover the Facts***: John gives more detail about Jesus' interaction with one particular woman, Mary Magdalene (v. 1), but we know from the other gospels that at least 3 other women were with her when they went to the tomb.

    What did Mary Magdalene tell Peter and John (v. 2)?

    What do Peter and John do and see for themselves (vv. 3-9)?

    What did they not understand?

    After the disciples left, what is said about Mary Magdalene (vv. 10-11)?

    When she saw the angels, what was her concern (vv. 12-13)?

    When she sees Jesus but doesn't recognize Him, what was still her concern (vv. 14-15)?

    What does this tell you about her?

    When she recognizes Jesus calling her name, what does she say and do (vv. 16-17)?

What does Jesus tell her to do (v. 17)?

Mary obeys. What news does she give (v. 18)?

Read John 20:19-31.

8. *Discover the Facts*: Jesus shows Himself to His disciples.

    On Sunday evening, the disciples were together in a room behind locked doors because they were afraid. Jesus came and stood among them and said, "Peace be with you!" Then what did He do (v. 20)? See also Luke 24:36-43.

    How did the disciples respond?

    What did Jesus reconfirm to them in v. 21 before temporarily giving them the Holy Spirit?

    Thomas missed Jesus' appearance. What was Thomas's response when the others told him about seeing Jesus (v. 25)?

    But what did Jesus do for Thomas a week later (vv. 26-27)?

    What is Thomas's response now (v. 28)?

    What is Jesus' response to Thomas that also applies to us (v. 29)?

    Write John 20:31 in the space below. This fits with Jesus' words in v. 29.

9. ***Heartbreak to Hope:*** Reflecting on John 20:29 (those of us who have not seen and yet believe). What drew you to believe in Jesus? When? Where? Who?

Respond to the Lord about what He's shown you today.

Day Four Study

Ask the Lord Jesus to speak to you through His Word. Tell Him that you are listening.

Read Luke 24:13-35.

10. ***Discover the Facts:*** Two men get a great sermon!

    As two men were walking the 7 miles from Jerusalem to Emmaus, what happened (vv. 13-16)?

    What did Jesus ask them (v. 17)?

    Who did they think Jesus was before He was crucified (v. 19)?

    What news did they receive (vv. 22-24)?

    How did Jesus respond to this (vv. 25-27)?

    What happened next (vv. 28-31)?

What did they say to each other (v. 32)?

Then, what did they do (vv. 33-35)?

Read Matthew 28:16-20.

11. ***Discover the Facts:*** The eleven disciples the eleven disciples went to Galilee, to the mountain where Jesus had told them to go. There they worshiped Him and listened to what He had to say.

    What did Jesus say was given to Him?

    What commission did Jesus give to those under His authority?

    What does He promise to all His followers who are being commissioned?

    > **Scriptural Insight:** Jesus' Resurrection Appearances
    > That Morning—The women (Mark 16:1-8; Matthew 28:1-10; John 20:1-18)
    > That Afternoon—Peter and the two men walking to Emmaus (Luke 24:13-35)
    > That Evening—The disciples minus Thomas (John 20:19-25; Luke 24:36-43)
    > One week later—The disciples plus Thomas (John 20:26-31)
    > In Galilee—7 disciples (John 21); to 500 at once and His brother James (1 Corinthians 15:1-7); and gives the Great Commission to all His followers (Matthew 28:16-20)

    Read "Whatever Happened to the Apostles" in the RESOURCES section for additional insight.

12. ***Heartbreak to Hope:*** What in today's study speaks to your heart?

13. **Heartbreak to Hope:** Reflect back on this whole study, seeing how people experiencing heartbreak, pain, or uncertainty found hope, healing and love. Which ones will you remember the most?

Write a prayer to God in response to what He has shown you in this study of Mark.

Recommended: Listen to the podcast "Made Alive—No Longer Dead" after doing this lesson to reinforce what you have learned. Use the following listener guide.

PODCAST LISTENER GUIDE

Made Alive…No Longer Dead

JESUS' RESURRECTION IS THE GREATEST SUPERNATURAL EVENT IN HUMAN HISTORY!

- The empty tomb and the appearances of Jesus together are powerful evidence of the fact of Jesus' resurrection. When the early Christians spoke of Jesus being raised from the dead, they were claiming that something happened to Jesus, which had happened to no one else ever! God raised His Son from the dead and gave Him a new physical body that would never die again.

- Do you know why Jesus had to rise from the dead? Why is the physical bodily resurrection of Jesus Christ essential to our faith?

WHAT THE RESURRECTION DID NOT MEAN

- The resurrection was **not** meant to prove life after death.

- The resurrection was **not** the appearance of Jesus' spirit or ghost. The term "resurrection" in that day and time meant receiving a new physical body after a time of death. It was never a way of talking about a ghost or spirit.

- The resurrection also does **not** directly prove that Jesus is God. But the resurrection declared that what He did in His life and in His death was the work of God's Son.

- Jesus had to rise from the dead because His resurrection had several purposes in the plan of God.

PURPOSE #1 FOR JESUS' RESURRECTION—TO ANNOUNCE THE BEGINNING OF THE KINGDOM

- The Jews expected the resurrection to happen before the kingdom was established. They just didn't know that it would be a two-stage process—first, the Messiah resurrected, then later everyone else. *Daniel 12:2-3; Isaiah 26:19; John 5:28-29*

PURPOSE #2 FOR JESUS' RESURRECTION—TO GIVE ALL BELIEVERS HOPE FOR OUR FUTURE.

We get hope from knowing about Jesus' resurrected body.

- What stayed the same? Jesus looked like a normal human (not glowing). He talked, walked and preached a sermon at the same time, and had memory. He referred to Himself as having flesh and blood, could be touched, and could use His hands to eat.

- What was different? Sometimes it was hard to recognize Him. Jesus could appear and disappear at will. His body was physically robust after being severely beaten and crucified.

- Jesus is reigning over His Kingdom from heaven as God-man UNTIL He returns to set up His kingdom on earth. *Acts 1:9-11*

Jesus' resurrection gives us hope for our future.

- The Bible teaches that when you as a believer die, you go immediately to be with Jesus. *Luke 23:43; Philippians 1:23; 2 Corinthians 5:8-9; John 17:24*

- You will be in God's hand, in a prepared place, where you will receive comfort and be recognizable. *Acts 7:59-60; John 14:2-3; Luke 16:19-31; Revelation 6:9-11*

- You will get a resurrected human body like His. Perfect, sinless, robust, and designed for eternal life.

PURPOSE #3 FOR JESUS' RESURRECTION—PROVIDING A SOLUTION TO OUR STATE OF SPIRITUAL DEATH.

The need for life

- All humans are born spiritually dead in need of life. *Ephesians 2:1-3, 12*

- Jesus said that He came to give us life, abundant and full. We are made alive in Christ and are a new creation from that moment onward. *John 3:3-6; 5:24; 10:10; Ephesians 2:5; 2 Corinthians 5:17*

Restoration of life by the indwelling Holy Spirit

- It is the Holy Spirit who makes our spirits alive through His presence. *John 14:16-17*

- Resurrection brings life. And this life of Christ is in you. "Christ in you" is a fact of your new existence. *Colossians 1:27*

- We are **made alive…no longer dead**. This begins a new adventure of learning how to live with Christ in us and depending upon Him to do anything of value.

You are made alive…no longer dead.

- Because of God's great love for us, you can know and live with confidence that God's life is now indwelling you forever. You are alive in Christ. Christ is alive in you. Now you can enjoy the life given to you by Christ Himself.

- The resurrection of Jesus Christ is the greatest event in human history. Life-changing. Life-giving. Because of His resurrection, we get eternal spiritual life now and the promise of eternal physical life in our future—a new physical body that far exceeds anything we have ever known here. And this same Jesus is in His physical human body in heaven waiting for us to join Him there some day. That's hope!

Let Jesus satisfy your heart with hope, healing, and love as you get to know Him and trust Him more each day.

> Get a peek at Lesson One of the next study in the "Adventure with Jesus" series, *Radical Acts*. See the Holy Spirit erupting in the lives of believers since the Church began.

Preview of "Radical Acts"

Listen to the Podcast: Get Fired Up and Ready for Adventure

> **Recommended:** Listen to the podcast "Get Fired Up and Ready for Adventure" as an introduction to the whole study.

THE RADICAL BLESSING OF THE HOLY SPIRIT

- On the day of Pentecost around 30 AD, the power of God poured forth on the followers of Jesus gathered in Jerusalem. The church of Jesus Christ was born—a radically new creation on Earth that never existed before.

- The Holy Spirit is a radical blessing to us. The definition of radical is "having a profound or far-reaching effect." Through the Spirit's transforming power in our lives, He changes the world immeasurably and irreversibly.

3 REASONS WHY YOU SHOULD STUDY THE BOOK OF ACTS

Reason to study Acts # 1. To understand how to live out your life in Christ.

- Acts is a book of history. The Spirit of God selected what He wanted us to know. The book of Acts is really the acts of Jesus Christ by His Spirit through His Church.

- Acts is a book of theology. You will see how theology is lived out, evidence for the inspiration of scripture, and proof that the gospel message has never changed.

- Acts is a book of biography and human relationships. You will see the fire of the Spirit erupting in the lives of people who are touched by the Spirit and changed forever.

Reason to study Acts #2. To connect with your spiritual heritage

- Gain a connection and appreciation for those who obeyed Jesus by spreading the gospel everywhere they went to reach people like you who never saw Jesus face-to-face but learned to believe in Him as Savior and Lord.

Reason to study Acts #3. Because you need spiritual adventure.

- Acts is a book of adventure. Within the history, theology, biography, and relationships, this marvelous book introduces us to adventure with Jesus Christ.

ADVENTURE WITH THE SPIRIT OF GOD

- According to the dictionary, adventure is "an unusual or exciting, typically hazardous, experience or activity." Our English word *adventure* comes from the Latin for "about to happen." What a way to look at life following Jesus—something's about to happen!

- In Acts, the adventure definitely includes the unexpected. Adventure rarely means easy. But it never means alone. The Holy Spirit is with you and me every day, forever.

WHO IS THE HOLY SPIRIT?

We can know these truths about the Holy Spirit.

- *The Holy Spirit is the breath of God.* We can't see Him. But the Bible confirms that He lives inside every believer.

- *The Holy Spirit is the third person of the Trinity.* Our God is one God but three persons. The Spirit is a personal being just as the Father and the Son are persons.

- *The Holy Spirit is central to salvation.* He convicts the unbeliever of sin and makes believers into new creations the moment we believe. He enters our spirits and seals us with Himself so our salvation is secure. He unites us with Christ and places us into the universal Body of Christ.

- *The Holy Spirit is the One who makes the Christian life possible.* He is the first gift we receive from God when we trust in Jesus for salvation. And all those wonderful spiritual treasures Paul writes about in Ephesians and his other letters are wrapped up and delivered by the Holy Spirit to us in a package deal the moment we are saved.

- *The Holy Spirit is the power for spiritual growth.* He enables us to understand the Bible and takes our prayer needs to God the Father, even when we can't. He fills us with Himself and transforms us from the inside out so that our character looks more like Jesus and our lifestyle glorifies God more and more.

- This firepower is inside us. Yet, we must choose to cooperate, consciously depending on the Holy Spirit when making decisions, facing temptations, in our relationships, and in how we respond to the Spirit's leading us.

GETTING FIRED UP FOR ADVENTURE

- Volcanoes form over hot spots in the earth's crust where a crack allows molten lava to flow to the surface. The Holy Spirit's work in our lives becomes our own "hot spots."

- Open your eyes to the evidence around you of the firepower of the Holy Spirit—your own Holy Spirit hot spots. We hope that this study will also spark in you a longing and expectation for the Holy Spirit's transforming power in your life as you learn what it means to live in daily dependence upon Jesus Christ. God's Spirit will get you fired up and ready for adventure as you follow Jesus daily.

Let Jesus satisfy your heart with His Spirit's transforming power. And say yes to a life of adventure with Him!

ent
Lesson 1: Getting Fired Up for Adventure

Acts 1:1-26

A.D. 30

Like the power of a volcano pouring forth fiery lava, the power of God poured forth on the followers of Jesus gathered in Jerusalem on the day of Pentecost around 33 A.D. Born that day was a **radically** new creation on earth that never existed before—the Church—born not by natural power but by supernatural power. And the power behind its existence is the Holy Spirit. The Holy Spirit is a **radical** blessing to every believer and to the world.

Radical = "having a profound or far-reaching effect"

That word "radical" is an interesting word. It is often associated with something bad, such as free radicals, radical groups, but if radical is used to mean a profound and far-reaching effect, that certainly describes the Holy Spirit. And that's good! Through the Spirit's transforming power in our lives, He changes the world immeasurably and irreversibly. We will see that *Radical Acts* is an appropriate name for our study of the book of Acts.

One of the biblical symbols for the Holy Spirit is "fire." And just as fiery lava and ash erupt from a volcano and flow out to build new land, the Holy Spirit's fire erupts through the lives of believers to build Jesus' Church. Within a few years, it was well established on planet Earth because men and women got fired up for adventure with the Spirit of God.

DAY ONE STUDY

Adventure with the Spirit

The book of Acts introduces us to adventure with the Spirit of God.

Adventure = "an unusual or exciting, typically hazardous, experience or activity"

What comes to mind when you think of adventure? How adventurous are you? You might not be naturally adventurous, especially the "typically hazardous" part.

Our English word "adventure" comes from the Latin for "about to happen." Yep. What a way to look at life following Jesus—something's about to happen! And it's usually not what you expect. I can verify that!

In Acts, the adventure definitely includes the unexpected. Miracles occur in strange places and strange ways. The Gentiles are included as equals to the Jews in the Church. An earthquake selectively releases prison chains. Unselfish behavior just springs forth in surprising ways. Add to that executions, beatings, riots, and a shipwreck—happening to the good guys! Adventure rarely means safe. But it never means alone. The Holy Spirit is with you and me every day, forever.

Who is the Holy Spirit?

But who is this Holy Spirit? Most Christians have only a vague idea about Him. The older translations called Him the Holy Ghost. The word "ghost" doesn't inspire appreciation or curiosity in me! In Greek, He is called the *pneuma*, meaning "the breath" of God. He's been called the transparent one because we can't see Him. The Bible confirms that He lives inside every believer. By faith, I know He lives in me. Sometimes, I feel His presence. Maybe you do too.

The Holy Spirit is the third person of the Trinity. Our God is one God but three persons. The Spirit is not an impersonal "it" or simply an influence but a personal being just as the Father and the Son are persons.

The Holy Spirit is central to salvation. He convicts the unbeliever of sin and makes believers into new creations the moment we believe. He seals us with Himself so our salvation is secure, and He indwells us forever. He unites us with Christ, placing us into the universal Body of Christ. We are all part of the one Church since Pentecost. That includes those who are already in heaven as well as every Christian alive at this moment.

The Holy Spirit is the One who makes the Christian life possible. He is the first gift we receive from God when we trust in Jesus for salvation. And all those wonderful treasures Paul writes about in Ephesians and his other letters are wrapped up and delivered by the Holy Spirit to us in a package deal the moment we are saved.

The Holy Spirit is the power for spiritual growth. He enables us to understand the Bible and prays for us, even when we can't. He fills us with Himself and transforms us from the inside out so that our character looks more like Jesus and our lifestyle glorifies God more and more. This firepower is inside us. Yet, we must choose to cooperate. That means living our lives with a conscious dependence on the Holy Spirit—when facing temptations, making decisions, in our relationships, and in how we respond to the Spirit's leading us. Trusting God in ways that you never did in the past, that's the adventure. You'll learn all about this in *Radical Acts*.

For a more detailed discussion of the Holy Spirit, including verses that support the above statements, see "Who Is the Holy Spirit?" in the RESOURCES section at the back of the book.

1. What did you learn about the Holy Spirit that you did not already know or appreciate?

The ABCs of Acts—Author, Background, and Context

Like any book you read, it always helps to know a bit about the author, the background setting for the story (i.e., past, present, future), and where the book fits into a series (that's the context). The same is true of Bible books.

AUTHOR

Although the author does not name himself, evidence from the text leads to the conclusion that the author was Luke, the physician and traveling companion of Paul (Colossians 4:14; 2 Timothy 4:11; Philemon 24). Certain passages using the pronoun "we" indicate the author includes himself as Paul's companion on his journeys. Some word choices in both Luke and Acts suggest that a medical man was the author of these books (Acts 28:6). The abrupt close indicates that Acts must have been finished around A.D. 62.

Background

The book of Acts is a fast-paced, action adventure book that chronicles the birth and growth of the early church from the Jewish center of Jerusalem to the Gentile nations surrounding her. It's a rich and fascinating book with something for everyone.

- Acts is a book of **history**. But it's not a complete history of the early church or the apostles but a selective history of early Christianity from Jesus' ascension through two years of Paul's Roman imprisonment. Some call it the Acts of the Apostles. But it's really the acts of Jesus Christ by His Spirit through His Church.

- Acts is a book of **theology**. Through His messengers, the Holy Spirit teaches people the truth about God and displays God's reality and power through miracles. You will see evidence for the inspiration of scripture and how the gospel message taught from the very beginning has never changed.

- Acts is a book of **biography.** It tells about the fire of the Spirit erupting in the lives of Peter, Paul, and their companions as well as many others whose lives were touched by the Spirit and changed forever.

- Acts is also a book about **human relationships** influenced by the transforming fire power of the Spirit. Conflicts occur and are resolved, friendships are made and tested, old prejudices surface and are removed, persecutions are shared, hospitality is extended, generosity is displayed, and opportunity taken to share the gospel with whomever would listen. Men and women got fired up and not only ready for adventure, but living the adventure with God.

Context

As a second volume to Luke's Gospel, the book of Acts provides a bridge for the writings of the New Testament, joining what Jesus "began to do and to teach" (Acts 1:1) as told in the Gospels with what he continued to do and teach through the apostles' preaching and the establishment of the church. It links the Gospel narratives with the apostolic letters that follow. It supplies an account of Paul's life from which we learn the settings for his letters. Geographically its story spans the lands between Jerusalem (where the church began) and Rome (the political center of the empire). Historically it recounts the first 30 years of the church. Within it are references to historical events occurring in the Roman Empire known from outside sources. It is also a bridge that ties the church in its beginning with each succeeding age.

2. What information did you learn from the ABC's of Acts that you did not already know?

> **Think About It:** Acts is a tribute to the transforming power of God, as seen in the Apostles' lives. Observing the changes in their lives from fearful weaklings to irrepressible dynamos gives us hope and encouragement today." (Sue Edwards, *Acts of the Holy Spirit,* p. 2)

Get Fired Up for Adventure

Our hope is that this study will spark in you a longing and expectation for the Holy Spirit's work in your life. We call those "hot spots." Through these lessons, you will discover who the Holy Spirit is, His intended role in your life, and what it means to live in daily dependence upon Him. He is the one who will work through that "hot spot" in your life and get you fired up for adventure as you follow Jesus daily.

> **Think About It:** "The work of God can only be carried on by the power of God. The church is a spiritual organism fighting spiritual battles. Only spiritual power can make it function as God ordained. The key is not money, organization, cleverness, or education. No matter the society or culture, the city or town, God has never lacked the power to work through available people to glorify His name … The times are urgent, God is on the move, now is the moment to ask God to ignite His fire in your soul!" (Jim Cymbala, *Fresh Wind, Fresh Fire*)

3. **Your Life Adventure:** Are you ready to get fired up for adventure with Jesus? What are you hoping to learn from this study?

Day Two Study

Recommended: Read Acts 1:1-26 to get the whole picture.

Read Luke 1:1-4.

4. **Discover the Facts:**

   Who handed down the information (v. 2)?

   What did Luke do (v. 3)?

   For what purpose (v. 4)?

> **Focus on the Meaning:** "Theophilus" means lover of God. Some interpreters have suggested that Theophilus was not an actual person and that Luke was writing to all lovers of God whom he personified by using this name (cf. Luke 1:3). All things considered, it seems more likely that Theophilus was a real person. There is no reason he could not have been. Such is the implication of the address, and Theophilus was a fairly common Greek proper name. (*Dr. Constable's Notes on Acts 2017 Edition*, p. 12)

5. Since Luke wrote the book of Acts, what confidence do you have that what you will be studying in Acts is trustworthy information?

Read Acts 1:1-3.

6. ***Discover the Facts:***

   What does the author say in vv. 1-2?

   After His suffering, what did Jesus do (v. 3)?

   From the Greek: The Greek word *tekmeriois*, translated "proofs," occurs only here in the New Testament. It refers to proof by incontrovertible evidence as contrasted with the proof claimed by a witness. Luke asserted that Jesus Christ's resurrection was beyond dispute. (*Dr. Constable's Notes on Acts 2017 Edition*, p. 13)

7. To what convincing proofs were the disciples a witness?

   - See Matthew 28:8-10—

   - Luke 24:36-42—

   - 1 Corinthians 15:5-7—

8. ***Your Life Adventure:*** Read John 20:26-29. What did Jesus say about those who have not seen Him in bodily form and still believe? Why should you count yourself as one of those "blessed" ones?

DAY THREE STUDY
Read Acts 1:1-11.
9. ***Discover the Facts***: Focus now on vv. 4-11.
    What was Jesus doing with them (v. 4)?

    Why were they to wait in Jerusalem (v. 4)?

    What would happen in a few days (v. 5)?

    What question did they ask Jesus (v. 6)?

    What is Jesus' answer in v. 7?

    What would they receive (v. 8 first part)?

    What would they then become (v. 8 second part)?

    What happened next (v. 9)?

    Who suddenly stood beside them (v. 10)?

    What did they promise (v. 11)?

Focus on the Meaning: The word translated "baptized" came from the process for "dyeing" cloth. It didn't matter if the cloth was sprayed, dipped, or immersed. The significance was taking on the identity of the dye. For us, the Spirit does the dyeing—with Jesus. We are dyed with Christ. Water baptism is a picture of what the Spirit does to us. John baptized with water; Jesus baptizes with the Spirit—much more significant and with far greater effects. See Romans 6.

10. Read the following verses to see what Jesus had promised them about the Spirit.

    - John 14:15-17—

    - John 16:12-15—

11. *Your Life Adventure:* What grabbed your attention in this passage? Reflect and respond to what the Holy Spirit pointed out for you to notice.

Day Four Study

Read Acts 1:12-26.

12. *Discover the Facts*:

    Where did they go after Jesus left them?

    Who was present there (vv. 13-14)?

    What were they doing (v. 14)?

    How many believers were there (v. 15)?

    What were the qualifications for filling Judas's vacant place (vv. 21-22)?

HEARTBREAK TO HOPE: GOOD NEWS FROM MARK

Whom did they propose (v. 23)?

What did they pray (vv. 24-25)?

Who was added to the Eleven (v. 26)?

Historical Insight: The practice of "casting lots" was common in the Old Testament (Proverbs 16:33), but this is the only recorded time the Apostles did this in the New Testament. Each candidate's name was written on a stone that was placed in a vessel and shaken. The first to fall out obtained the office. (Sue Edwards, *Acts of the Holy Spirit*, p. 6)

13. What did Peter already see as the set purpose for the apostles (v. 22)?

14. Whereas men and women were usually segregated in the synagogue, what were men and women doing together in this upper room (v. 14)?

Scriptural Insight: The women possibly included the wives of the apostles (1 Co 9:5) and those listed as ministering to Jesus (Mt 27:55; Lk 8:2-3; 24:22). (NIV Study Bible, p. 1644)

15. *Your Life Adventure:* The believers were joined together learning how to live dependently on Jesus for guidance. What did they do that you can also do?

Think About It: In this first chapter, three key elements of the book of Acts are introduced: 1) the emphasis on the many witnesses to Jesus' life, death and resurrection; 2) the Holy Spirit's guidance and empowering of believers, and 3) the dependent hearts of those same believers as they prayed. Keep these elements in mind as you work through the study.

GET FIRED UP FOR ADVENTURE:

16. **Hot Spot:** Where in this lesson did the Spirit grab your attention especially? What did you see Him do in your life this week?

> **Recommended:** Listen to the podcast "Trusting Jesus When Making Decisions" after doing this lesson to reinforce what you have learned. Use the following listener guide.

Trusting Jesus When Making Decisions

MAKING DECISIONS IS PART OF LIFE.

- Making decisions is part of daily life. We can't get away from it.

- What we have to learn is how to make those decisions in a way that maintains our dependence on Jesus Christ in the process. Jesus' followers had to learn that as well.

CASTING LOTS WAS A CULTURAL TOOL NOT A FORMULA.

- The practice of "casting lots" was common in the Old Testament. And God even used it to give direction to His people. This is the only record of its New Testament use.

- Casting lots as a cultural tool that God used with His people sometimes. He also used prophets and counsellors. *Proverbs 16:33*

- Casting lots was not a formula then nor is it a formula today. What we read in Acts is simply a description of what they did not a prescription for how to make decisions today.

DESCRIPTIVE VERSUS PRESCRIPTIVE

- Much of the Bible is written in narrative form. Narrative is usually descriptive not prescriptive.

- *Descriptive* means it is observation of what actually happened, how people lived and the choices they made about how to do life at the time.

- *Prescriptive* refers to commands from God about how to live or do something that applies to all believers, all people groups, and all time periods.

- We can't look at this passage in Acts chapter 1 about casting lots and create a formula for making decisions with God's blessing on the result.

- We also know that the Holy Spirit now lives inside every believer and can give us direction from the inside of our own hearts and minds for making decisions.

- From our study of Acts 1, we can look at the process the apostolic leaders used and see that the same process applies to us.

THE PROCESS FOR MAKING DECISIONS

Step 1. They aligned themselves with the purposes of God.

- Since Jesus had originally chosen 12 to represent the tribes of Israel, they would fill that 12th spot for the purpose that Jesus had set before them. It was a position of leadership to fill. They aligned themselves with the purposes of God.

Step 2. They considered options who were also aligned with the purposes of God.

- They used their own observations and mental acuity to evaluate the choices. Two men were equally good choices, and both were aligned with the purposes of God.

Step 3. They asked the Lord Jesus for His direction and for Him to show them the best choice.

- In the New Testament writings after the gospels, whenever you see "the Lord," that refers to Jesus. God is God the Father, Lord is the Lord Jesus Christ, and the Spirit is the Holy Spirit.

- The disciples submitted their options to their Lord Jesus and asked for Him to show them which to choose. *"Lord, you know everyone's heart. Show us which of these two you have chosen (Acts 1:24)*

- This is living dependently on God. God the Father who is also your Creator has given you a brain to use. He wants you to use your mind and heart to evaluate the options and then remove the options that are not lined up with His way of doing life. Once you have done that, ask the Lord to show you which good option to choose. It is an act of faith.

Step 4. They submitted to Jesus' direction for them.

- They asked for God to show them, and God did. Then, they submitted to that. Matthias became the 12th apostle and joined the leader team.

DECISION-MAKING AS PART OF DEPENDENT LIVING

- Decision-making is a huge part of dependent living. What decision do you need to make this week? Follow those guidelines I just gave you, trusting Jesus with your decision-making.

Let Jesus satisfy your heart with His Spirit's transforming power. And say yes to a life of adventure with Him!

Get *Radical Acts* at melanienewton.com as well as most online bookstores.

The Miracles of Jesus in Mark

Miracle	Passage	Demonstrated	Response
Cure of demon possessed man in synagogue	1:21-28	Jesus' authority over what he did and in how he taught	The people were amazed.
Healing of Peter's mother-in-law	1:29-31	Jesus' compassion to Peter and Peter's family	Peter's mother-in-law rose from the bed and began serving her guests.
Healing of a leper	1:40-45	Jesus' compassion for the man; his not being bound by Mosaic Law regarding defilement; and testified to his divine power.	Instead of obeying Jesus by remaining silent and presenting himself to the priests, the man who was healed went out spreading the new.
Healing a paralyzed man	2:1-12	Jesus' authority on earth to forgive sin.	The man got up, took his mat, and walked away as Jesus had commanded.
Healing a man with a withered hand	3:1:5	Jesus is Lord of the Sabbath.	The Pharisees went away plotting Jesus' death.
Calming the storm on the Sea of Galilee	4:35-41	Jesus demonstrated his sovereign power.	The disciples were in awe of what had been done but they still did not understand who Jesus is as is expressed when they ask the question, "Who is this?"
The healing of a demon-possessed man	5:1-20	Jesus' divine origin and superior power	The townspeople were fearful of further financial loss and requested that Jesus leave them. The cured man begged to go with Jesus, but Jesus told him to go home and tell his family what the Lord had done for him. He went in the Decapolis (a league of free cities) and told people what Jesus had done. Everyone who heard was amazed.
Raising Jairus's daughter	5:22-43	Jesus' authority over death	Ordered the parents and three disciples (John, Peter, James) to silence and that the girl be fed.
Healing a woman who was hemorrhaging	5:25-34	Jesus' ability to distinguish the touch of one who has faith and expects deliverance.	Woman approached Jesus with reverence to his response to come forward.

Miracle	Passage	Demonstrated	Response
Feeding the 5,000	6:32-44	Jesus' being God incarnate (Ezekiel 34:23-31 – God promised that when the true Shepherd came the desert would become a fertile pasture where the sheep would gather and be well-fed. Ps. 23:1 – "The Lord is my Shepherd, I shall not want").	The disciples did not understand who Jesus was.
Walking on water	6:45-52	Jesus' true identity as God.	Disciples were amazed and their hearts were hardened
Casting out a demon of a Syrophoenician woman's daughter	7:24-30	Jesus' grace and being able to perform a miracle without physically being present.	Woman demonstrated her personal faith in Jesus.
Healing of a deaf mute	7:31-37	Fulfillment of God's healings during Messianic age as stated in Old Testament. (Isa 35:5-6 – "the ears of the deaf unstopped....and the mute tongue shout for joy.")	The people were overwhelmed and amazed and continuously talked about the healing even when Jesus commanded them not to do so.
Feeding the 4,000	8:1-9	Jesus' compassion	Disciples still did not understand that Jesus would provide for all.
Healing of a blind man of Bethsaida	8:22-26	Jesus is doing what God had promised in Old Testament. (Isa 35:5 – "Then will the eyes of the blind be opened..."	Man was healed and went home.
The healing of a boy with and evil spirit	9:14-29	Lack of dependency on God's power through prayer by the disciples	Disciples questioned why they couldn't drive the demon out when they knew that they had been given the ability to heal.
Healing of Bartimaeus who was blind	10:46-52	Bartimaeus's recognition that Jesus was the true Messiah of Israel	Bartimaeus's faith healed him and he became a follower.

Principles on Marriage and Divorce

Principle #1: God created male and female in the beginning. Genesis 1:26-28

Men and women were created individually in the image of God. Both together were given the first command to mankind in the Bible—to flourish, to fill the earth with their kind, and to exercise dominion and stewardship over the earth including the other earthly creatures.

Principle #2: Marriage is one man and one woman united for life. Genesis 2:18, 24-25; Matthew 19:4-6

In the beginning, God chose to create and bring together the first man and woman in marriage. The man and woman were from then on to leave their parents, form a covenant with one another, and unite into a new family unit, no longer under the protective custody of their parents. God gives men and women the freedom to choose their own marriage partners following the pattern and instructions He gave for the next generations.

Being "united" refers to an inseparable union of which sexual intercourse is a picture. They are no longer two, but one. Since this is by God's design, when a man and woman marry, forming that fleshly union, they are under God's authority ("God has joined together"). According to Jesus, neither the man nor the woman nor any other human is to separate (Greek *chorizeto* = "divorce") them.

Principle #3: Divorce is opposite God's covenantal nature. Malachi 2:13-16

As sin affected the God/man relationship, it also infiltrated and infected human-to-human relationships, including marriage. Divorce breaks a covenant of which God is the witness so is opposite God's faithful nature. As God stayed faithful to His covenant partner, Israel, so should a husband/wife stay faithful to his/her marriage partner.

One of the purposes of marriage is to provide an environment to produce godly offspring. Separating a married couple through divorce may reduce this opportunity as it brings "violence" to the family. God hates divorce the same as He hates other sin such as haughty eyes, a lying tongue, hands that kill the innocent, a heart that plots evil, feet that race to do wrong, a false witness who pours out lies, and a person who sows discord among brothers. (Proverbs 6:16-19, same Hebrew word)

Principle #4: Before Christ, divorce was permitted to control the consequences of man's sin. Matthew 19:8; Deuteronomy 22:23, 24

God divinely provided a way to deal with situations brought about by men's hard hearts toward their wives and to protect from its worst effects those who would suffer as a result of it. Throughout the Old Testament are such provisions made to limit and control the consequences of man's sinfulness (the cities of refuge, for example). Legal divorce is better than desertion. It appears that the divorced spouse is not condemned in this case.

Principle #5: Since marriage is a physical union, only a physical cause can break it such as death or fornication. Romans 7:1-3; Matthew 5:32; 19:9

Marital unfaithfulness could include adultery committed during the marriage or betrothal period, illegitimate marriages (incestuous ones), or a relentless persistent lifestyle of unfaithfulness (prostitution, pornography). Although adultery was punishable by death, occupation by the Romans prevented this from being carried out in Jesus' day. Since the marriage covenant is already broken by one spouse, the faithful spouse has permission to seek a divorce and is free to marry again without it being considered adultery. It appears that divorce in this case is not considered sin for the violated spouse. Under Roman law, a wife could divorce her husband. Under traditional Jewish law, she could not.

Principle #6: Two Christians who are married to one another are to remain married. If they divorce, they are to remain unmarried or be reconciled. 1 Corinthians 7:10-11

The controlling principle throughout this chapter (1 Corinthians 7) in Paul's letter is to "Stay as you are" when you become a Christian. Paul confirms what Jesus already stated in Matthew 19. Those believers who are already married to one another must recognize the permanence of their commitment, as was taught by the Lord Jesus, and not seek divorce. If they do divorce, each is to remain unmarried or be reconciled. Does the exception of marital unfaithfulness apply to believers? Yes, because the covenant is broken in a physical way. However, reconciliation and forgiveness is the better way.

> Adultery does not mandate divorce, but God does allow divorce as a consequence of adultery. It's even better for the unfaithful spouse to repent, for the violated spouse to forgive and for them to forge a new, stronger relationship. This isn't always possible due to the hardness of some people's hearts, and God understands and allows for it. (Sue Bohlin, *Probe Answers Questions about Specifics*, "Am I Committing Adultery?")

Principle #7: A Christian with a non-Christian spouse is to remain married unless the unbeliever is unwilling to live with his/her Christian spouse. Then, the believer should release him/her in peace and is free to remain single or to remarry another Christian only. 1 Corinthians 7:12-15, 39

Once again, the controlling principle throughout this chapter in Paul's letter is to "Stay as you are" when you become a Christian if possible. Jesus did not specifically address this situation in His teachings, but Paul based his response on Jesus' teaching on marriage and human relationships in general. If the unbelieving spouse does not object to the husband/wife becoming a Christian and is willing to remain married, they are to do so.

The unbeliever may be saved through the witness of the believing spouse. (1 Corinthians 7:14; 1 Peter 3:1-2) God will be actively working in that house because His child is in that house. The goal is for the Christian spouse to preserve the marriage union and live "in peace" with the non-Christian, but with the understanding that marriage is a mutual not a unilateral relationship.

However, the unbeliever may also continue to reject Christ. In the case of an unbelieving spouse not willing to live with a husband/wife who has become a Christian, the Christian is to let the unbeliever free. Don't live in turmoil because of it. Divorce initiated by the unbeliever on these grounds is not condemned.

Principle #8: A Christian whose spouse has died is free to remain single or to remarry another Christian only. 1 Corinthians 7:39

Since death breaks the covenant, the widow or widower is completely free to remarry, provided that the new spouse is a believer.

Principle #9: Singleness is a gift from God and demands sexual purity. 1 Corinthians 7:7-9

In Jewish law, marriage was obligatory for all men except the sexually impotent. Being enabled to be married or to stay single is considered a gift of God. "Satisfied singleness" is good. The one who is unsatisfied to refrain from sexual experience as a single should recognize that God has gifted them for marriage. Neither being a chaste single nor being a faithful married partner is a higher calling. Neither staying single nor getting married is sin.

Sources:

1. *Dr. Tom Constable's Notes on Mark*
2. Walvoord and Zuck, *The Bible Knowledge Commentary, Old Testament*
3. Walvoord and Zuck, *The Bible Knowledge Commentary, New Testament*
4. Tim Stevenson, *First Letter of Paul to the Corinthians,* pages 7.1-7.4
5. Sue Bohlin, *Probe Answers Questions about Specifics,* "Am I Committing Adultery?"

Whatever Happened to the Twelve Apostles?

The New Testament tells of the fate of only two of the apostles: Judas (Iscariot), who betrayed Jesus and then went out and hanged himself, and James the son of Zebedee, who was executed by Herod about 44 A.D. (Acts 12:2). As to the rest of the apostles, reports and legends abound, though not always reliable, but still giving us some clue as to what might have happened. An early legend says they cast lots and divided up the world to determine who would go where, so all could hear about Jesus. They suffered greatly for their faith and in most cases met violent deaths on account of their bold witness.

PETER and PAUL were both executed in Rome about 66 A.D., during the persecution under Emperor Nero. Paul was beheaded. Peter was crucified upside down, at his request, since he did not feel he was worthy to die in the same manner as his Lord.

ANDREW went to the "land of the man-eaters," in what is now the Soviet Union. Christians there claim him as the first to bring the gospel to their land. He also preached in Asia Minor (modern-day Turkey) and in Greece, where it is thought he was crucified.

THOMAS was probably most active in the area east of Syria. Tradition has him preaching in India, where the ancient Marthoma Christians revere him as their founder and claim that he died there when pierced through with the spears of four soldiers.

PHILIP possibly had a powerful ministry in Carthage in North Africa and then in Asia Minor, where the wife of a Roman proconsul accepted the gospel. In retaliation, the proconsul had Philip arrested and cruelly put to death.

MATTHEW the tax collector and writer of the Gospel bearing his name, ministered in Persia and Ethiopia. Some of the oldest reports say he was not martyred, while others say he was stabbed to death in Ethiopia.

BARTHOLOMEW (also known as Nathaniel) had widespread missionary travels attributed to him by tradition: to India with Thomas, back to Armenia, and also to Ethiopia and Southern Arabia. There are various accounts of how he met his death as a martyr for the gospel.

JAMES the son of Alphaeus, is one of at least three James referred to in the New Testament. This James is reckoned to have ministered in Syria. The Jewish historian Josephus reported that he was stoned and then clubbed to death.

SIMON THE ZEALOT, so the story goes, ministered in Persia and was killed after refusing to sacrifice to the sun god.

Little is known of Thaddaeus (also known as Judas, not Iscariot).

MATTHIAS was the apostle chosen to replace Judas. Tradition sends him to Syria with Andrew and to death by burning.

JOHN is the only one of the company generally thought to have died a natural death from old age. He was the leader of the church in Ephesus. During Domitian's persecution in the middle 90's, he was exiled to the island of Patmos. There he wrote the last book of the New Testament—Revelation. An early Latin tradition has him escaping unhurt after being cast into boiling oil at Rome.

Sources

1. *Answers Magazine*, Vol. 2 No. 3, "Biblical Leprosy: Shedding Light on the Disease that Shuns"
2. *Dr. Constable's Notes on Mark 2017 Edition*
3. *Dr. Constable's Notes on Matthew 2017 Edition*
4. Lisa Jenkins-Moore, "Entwined in Him," *Living Magazine,* November 2016
5. *NIV Study Bible 1984 Edition*, Zondervan
6. N.T. Wright, *Jesus and the Victory of God: Christian Origins and the Question of God, Volume 2*
7. Rodger C. Young, *Book review: From Abraham to Paul: A Biblical Chronology, by Andrew E. Steinmann,* accessed online
8. Sue Bohlin, *Probe Answers Questions about Specifics,* "Am I Committing Adultery?"
9. Walvoord and Zuck, *The Bible Knowledge Commentary, New Testament,*
10. Walvoord and Zuck, *The Bible Knowledge Commentary, Old Testament,*
11. Tim Stevenson, *First Letter of Paul to the Corinthians*
12. "What does Messiah mean?" accessed at gotquestions.org
13. Woven, *The Truth about Redemption Next Step,* "Redeeming Hope: Your journey Toward Surrender"

Made in United States
Orlando, FL
02 January 2025